Abandoned

Abandoned

The true story of a
little girl who didn't belong

ANYA PETERS

This is a work of non-fiction. In order to protect privacy,
some names and places have been changed.

HarperElement
An Imprint of HarperCollins*Publishers*
77–85 Fulham Palace Road
Hammersmith, London W6 8JB

The website address is: www.thorsonselement.com

and *HarperElement* are trademarks of
HarperCollins*Publishers* Limited

Published by HarperElement 2007

1 3 5 7 9 10 8 6 4 2

A catalogue record for this book is
available from the British Library

ISBN-13 978-0-00-724572-7
ISBN-10 0-00-724572-6

Printed in Great Britain by
Clays Ltd, St Ives plc

This book is proudly printed on paper which contains wood
from well-managed forests, certified in accordance with
the rules of the Forest Stewardship Council.
For more information about FSC,
please visit www.fsc.org

To Mummy,
whose love was always there
as the dock leaf to soothe the sting of him ...
And to Brendan, for never letting go.

'Although the world is full of suffering,
it is full also of the overcoming of it.'
(Helen Keller, 1880–1968)

Acknowledgements

Thank you to everyone who made this book possible. To my agent, Camilla Hornby, for having the vision to see this as a book at a time when I was only brave enough to write it as scattered suggestions throughout a blog. To my patient and enthusiastic editors, Sally Potter and Susanna Abbott, and the dedicated team at HarperElement for taking a chance on me and for making this happen. And to Andrew Crofts for help in bringing my story to life.

Thanks, too, to *New York Times* journalist, Ian Urbina, and Sean Coughlan of BBC News Online magazine for shining their light down into my laneway when I so much needed it. And to the bloggers everywhere, whose encouragement, support and compassion helped me through the darkest months, and to believe in myself again.

For those whose practical help I was so grateful for: to Hugh for the sleeping bag; to Reverend Jim for the bag of food that got me through a bank holiday weekend I don't know how I would have got through otherwise; for the replacement St Christopher that was sent to me poste restante, and for all the other help that seemed to turn up just when I was most in need of it. I hope all your kindnesses come back to you many times over.

Abandoned

To all those people who are still locked in their own chains of abuse. I hope this book comes into some of your hands, and that my story gives you hope that there *are* second chances – that however impossible it seems, you can survive and can move on.

Lastly, and especially, to Claire and Sunil for coming when you did. To the other Andrew, for not turning your back when you were the first one I got back in touch with and told about this book and how I had been living; for the bolthole in Cornwall and all those long drives down; and for chocolate and your faith in me. I am very grateful. Love and thanks to Kate, also, for getting back in touch, and for all the late-night phone calls and the best margaritas. And to Alex, for reminding me of the Emerson quote you stuck to the side of my computer: 'Our greatest glory consists not in never falling, but in rising every time we fall.'

Chapter 1

It's after an argument. Mummy stands at the kitchen table counting out plates. It's roast chicken, which means it's a Sunday. And I know it's after an argument because she calls Daddy 'him'.

She runs through us all in her head, tapping out numbers against her palm, then slides that number of plates along the counter from the stack she has taken from the shelf.

'Wait … who have I missed?'

I look up, nervous that it's me. My two eldest sisters, Marie and Sandra, aren't there that day so there should be seven.

'Him, Michael, Liam, Stella, Jennifer, you, me,' she says, counting us out again by name.

She always counts the plates out like that, in that order: almost by ages, except she puts the girls before me, and herself at the end. I like the way she puts me with her at the end, the way she says, '… you, me …' Always like that.

Mummy never leaves me out; she treats us all the same, but every mealtime I'm waiting for the same thing, for there to be one plate short, or not enough of something to go around. And for my uncle, or even one of the others imitating him, to look around at me and say, 'She can do without. She doesn't belong here anyway.'

Abandoned

It's what Daddy is always saying, screaming it out week after week in drunken arguments.

'She's not wanted here, right! She doesn't belong here. I want her out.'

I feel my brothers and sisters stiffen on the settee beside me, rolling their eyes at each other. I know they're all thinking the same thing: thinking that I'm the trouble-maker; wishing I wasn't there; that Daddy wouldn't shout and argue half as much if I wasn't, that they could watch TV in peace.

'She's not wanted. They dumped her over here with you because they didn't want her over there and she's not wanted here either. I want her out,' he says, snapping open another beer, 'she doesn't belong here.'

I hold my nose to stop the tears, trying to lean back behind the others on the settee so he can't see me, staring hard at the wires at the back of the TV, not daring to watch the screen in case something on it triggers my tears. He'll hit me harder if he sees me crying. He always does.

'She's only a child; none of this is her fault. Leave her alone, you bully. Go and pick on someone your own size. She's no trouble at all. This is my home, and if I want her here, she'll stay,' Mummy yells in the background.

I wish she would just stop, not argue back. Mummy is worn out trying to stand up for me – but usually she just makes it worse.

'She's wanted nowhere, right!'

'Yes she is, you cruel drunk … Don't listen to him, Anya.'

But I have to.

'Why did they leave her over here then? Who wants her?' he screams. 'No one!' he says louder, slamming the words into me.

Abandoned

'Yes they do! I want her!' Mummy hollers into the room.

I try everything to keep my tears in, but eventually they burst out, hiccupping as they come, my shoulders heaving, and he is over me, his fist raised, ready to give me 'something to really cry about'.

Chapter 2

Mummy wasn't my real mum. Her younger sister, Katherine, who everyone called 'Kathy', was my real mum. I can't remember a time when I didn't know that. Anyway, my uncle, who I grew up calling 'Daddy' like the rest of my brothers and sisters, would never have allowed it to be kept a secret. He took every opportunity to remind me that Mummy wasn't my real mum, that I didn't belong with them, and that any day I'd be sent over 'to that whore of a mother of yours in Ireland'.

Kathy was twelve years younger than Mummy, and beautiful. She was slim and elegant, with long, soft-red curls like shiny new pennies down her back, and eyes that were almost navy blue. She had the tiniest hands I, or any of my brothers and sisters, had ever seen on a grown-up, little doll's hands, with long oval nails always painted a deep dark red. I was fascinated by her: by her beauty and calmness and easy laughter, by her soft Irish accent and her gentleness with me. But I was fearful of her too, always on my guard with her, determined to keep her at a distance. Determined to let Mummy see that she was my mum, not her sister Kathy.

For years Kathy wore a heavy, gold charm bracelet that clattered noisily at her wrist, and on each visit there'd be a new charm or two. My brothers and sisters would gather around her, choosing their favourite. One of my earliest memories is watching, out of the corner of my eye, my brother Liam sitting in stripy pyjamas in her arms as we all watch TV in the small front room of our flat. He holds up her bare arm and sleepily goes through the charms one by one, trying to choose his favourite between a miniature of the Houses of Parliament and a cat with tiny, diamond-encrusted eyes. I watch her small hand stroking the back of his blond head, her red curls falling down across his chest, and feel suddenly cold and stiff, too young to put words to the mixture of jealously and hate I feel as I look on. I am eight months younger than Liam, but my uncle doesn't allow anyone to hold or touch me like that.

Kathy lived at home with her and Mummy's parents in Ireland, but I was born in England, on one of the beds in the long back bedroom in Mummy's flat. But ten days after I was born she had to go back to Ireland, and left me there for Mummy to look after.

It was only supposed to be a temporary arrangement, just until the day she could come back to get me. But that day never came. She did come back – four or five times a year on visits – but she never took me with her, though every visit I was terrified that she might, that my uncle's constant threats that 'this' time he was going to see to it that she took her 'baggage' back with her would be carried out.

Mummy had three other sisters. She was the eldest and Kathy was the youngest, still a child at the time Mummy left Ireland to make a life for herself over in England, and the only one left at home to look after their parents if ever they needed it.

She hadn't even had a boyfriend before she met my father. I didn't know who he was but I soon found out that he was a married man, and that they had been having an affair. Mummy told me that much one night after my uncle had stormed off to bed following one of their drunken arguments. My brothers and sisters had been herded off to bed earlier in the evening, but, as he often did, my uncle made me sit there and listen. It was on those nights, once he'd gone to bed, and before my brothers and sisters tiptoed back down one by one, that Mummy would tell me all her stories about growing up in Ireland.

Sometimes when we were on our own she would tell me stories about Kathy, and how she came over to England on her own on the ferry to have me in London, stories that only part of me wanted to hear. But layer by layer, argument by argument, year by year, as I, or more usually my brothers and sisters, asked more questions, I pieced together the details of my life story.

Mummy always made the stories sound romantic and exciting and sad, and we all felt sorry for Kathy not being able to be with her baby or with the man she had fallen in love with. I tried to forget that I was the baby they were talking about.

My feelings towards Kathy were always complicated, but I was shocked when I found out my father was a married man. In those days, extra-marital affairs were absolutely taboo. I looked at Kathy differently after that. I blamed her even more for the trouble Mummy was going through to keep her 'secret' for her, and for being the centre of most of the drunken arguments in our home.

'She loved your father very much,' Mummy always told me during those talks, 'I know that much.'

I would pretend I wasn't interested in the bits about Kathy and who my father might be. As usual I wanted to show Mummy that it was *her* I wanted to be my mum, not her sister; that *this* was my family and that I never wanted to be taken away from them. But of course I always did listen. I listened hard.

'Did you know who Anya's dad was?' my youngest sister Jennifer asked one night.

We'd all asked the same question over the years. I pretended not to hear, but when I glanced up I saw Mummy look away and shake her head, and her eyes filled with tears again.

'No,' she said, swirling the drink in her glass and staring into it, 'no I didn't.'

'Would you tell Daddy if you did?' I asked.

'Yes,' she said, pulling the belt of her dressing gown tighter and knocking back the last of her drink. 'You bet your life I would. I wouldn't put up with what I take from that madman … not even for my sister.'

Chapter 3

My uncle hated me being there. From the start he wanted me out. And the main purpose of my early years was to try to make myself as silent and as invisible as possible so that he would forget about me, and let me stay, to be part of the family I saw as my own.

He must have agreed to me being there at the beginning, but it was only ever meant to be a temporary arrangement. And his hatred of me grew as week by week, month by month it became more and more obvious that I was there to stay.

What he hated most was not being told who my 'real' father was. He was convinced that Mummy knew the truth and was keeping it a secret from him on the instructions of Kathy and her colleague from work – who was the only person in Ireland to know about her illegitimate child, and who we grew up knowing as our 'Uncle Brendan'. He thought they didn't trust him and that Mummy was lying for them.

Over and over through the years, Mummy shouted back at him that she *wasn't* lying, that she *didn't* know who my father was.

'If I knew, don't you think I would have told you by now?' she'd scream, sobbing.

But he knew that Kathy and Brendan didn't like him, particularly Brendan, and he called Mummy a liar, swearing that they were all taking him for a fool in his own home. The fact that no one would tell him drove him mad and seemed to be the spark for most of their rows.

She tried all sorts of answers on him, all sorts of ways of saying she didn't know, and, as I grew up, that I didn't know either – that I didn't have a father, that I'd been conceived in the course of a one-night stand. He never believed her. But because of it he called Kathy a 'whore', and me her 'whore's child', screaming it out in drunken argument after drunken argument throughout my childhood.

'My sister is *not* a whore,' Mummy would scream back.

'Who's the father then? Who's the father?' he shouted, over and over again, maddened that Kathy expected him to have me brought up under his roof, but still wouldn't trust him enough to tell him who my father was. 'I don't want their dirty work, their left-behinds, their whore's child in my house,' he'd shout. 'They can take her back over there with them where she belongs. And I'll make sure of it this time.'

It was the same every weekend. Usually, when Mummy managed to send me up to bed with the rest of them – even if I was yelled back down again later and forced to sit there and listen to it – we'd lie there listening to them raging at each other, and to Mummy being hit defending her sister and fighting for me to stay. When he finally stormed off to bed himself, Mummy would sometimes creep to the long back bedroom that the five youngest of us shared, to see if we were all right. Despite her assurances, I still thought with every argument that this time it would happen, that he would see to it that I was sent from my family, over to Kathy in Ireland, who was almost a stranger to us then – the 'whore', whose visits I dreaded.

We didn't have a dictionary at home – ours was a house without books – but when I was old enough, 'whore' was the first word I remember trying to look up in the big, blue-leather dictionary in our school library. I knew it wasn't a good word and that I couldn't ask our teacher, but I was desperate to find out exactly what Kathy was, and what a 'whore's child' actually meant. Nervous in case anyone saw me, I sat on the stripy window seat overlooking the playground with my back to everyone, turning the fragile, India paper quietly, with my heart hammering. But I didn't find out. I was looking under the 'H's', assuming it was spelt as it sounded. Not realising that it was hiding amongst the 'W's' at the end of the dictionary, as if ashamed of itself.

I never understood why Kathy wouldn't tell my uncle who my father was, and, as a child, I never forgave her for it. But then she didn't know exactly how violent and abusive he became. And she could never have imagined just how bad it was going to get.

Kathy knew the *type* of man he was, and maybe hoped that since they weren't married he and Mummy wouldn't stay together long. She wouldn't have wanted to give him any information he could later use against her if they did split up. She and her lover would never have survived the scandal if news of their affair got out in Ireland, and my uncle would have known that. If he had been able to find out who my father was, he might well have blackmailed him, or just told his wife and family what he knew. He was always threatening to write to my grandparents to tell them that Kathy had 'stashed her bastard' in London with them.

'What would your mum and dad say if they knew about me?' I asked one night after my uncle had drained the last of his vodka and staggered up to bed, leaving us all huddled around her in the aftermath of one of his rages.

'It'd kill them,' she said, 'literally, kill them.'

The others giggled and I swung my eyes away, shivering the words out of me one by one as I counted the twists of ivy repeated in the pattern of the curtain hanging across our back bedroom door. I tried hard not to imagine the grandparents I'd only ever heard stories about, dying just through knowing that I was alive.

Chapter 4

Kathy was only nineteen when she fell pregnant with me, and neither she nor her married lover knew what they were going to do. Because their affair had to remain a secret she had no one she could talk to about it either. Even if my father hadn't been a married man, life would not have been easy for an unmarried girl who found herself pregnant in the small-town Ireland of the early 1970s. Everyone was still under the fist of the Catholic Church at the time, and unmarried mothers, I was always told as a child, were still being put away in sanatoriums, their babies taken from them and put up for adoption as soon as they were born. Many chose instead to catch the boat to England or America, to have their babies and start brand-new lives.

When she could no longer conceal her pregnancy, Kathy came to England to find her eldest sister. Mummy had lost touch with her family, but Kathy knew she was living somewhere in London. While she was in Ireland, Mummy was the only one who had ever found out that Kathy was having an affair with a married man.

'Don't come crying to me when he gets you pregnant,' was the last thing she warned Kathy, washing her hands of it before she left for England.

'I won't,' Kathy said.

But two and a half years later, that was exactly what she did.

By that time it wasn't easy to find her sister in London because she'd moved several times without giving any of the family her new address. She'd divorced too, something that would have brought disgrace on her family in the Ireland of the time, and would have been the main reason for not keeping in touch with them. But somehow Kathy found her.

Years later, Kathy told me she was sure she must have had the wrong address when, late one evening, she turned up at the one she'd scribbled on the back of her ferry ticket: a block of flats in the middle of a sprawling, red-brick council estate in a run-down part of East London. She walked up the dark stairwell to the second floor landing and knocked on the red front door, half hoping her sister didn't live there. But when her sister opened it, with Michael – who was a toddler by then – hanging off one arm, and rocking an even younger child, who she'd had illegitimately, in the other, Kathy realised why her sister had lost touch with her family. She knew then that she would help keep her secret from their parents because, staring at baby Liam, she saw that her sister had been keeping secrets of her own.

I'm not sure what Kathy planned to do once she came over to England. Maybe she was going to have an abortion and her sister or her conscience talked her out of it. Maybe her lover did. Maybe she believed he would leave his wife and his 'empty-shell' marriage, as I was later told it was, and come over to take care of her and her baby in London. Or maybe she was going to have me no matter what.

Fate made the decision for them in the end. A telegram arrived, two weeks before I was due to be born. It was from her father. And it ruined everything. Her mother had suffered a serious stroke and the outlook wasn't good. Until that moment, post had been going only one way, with Kathy sending ever-briefer letters and postcards home, trying to edit out any clues, while making excuse after excuse for extending her holiday.

There can't be too many excuses you can use for extending a holiday when a telegram arrives bringing news of your mother's illness, but they had no choice but to rustle another one up; this time a broken leg which hadn't reset properly. For all they knew, though, their mother could have been on her deathbed. They couldn't phone to find out because neither Mummy nor her parents had a telephone then. But whatever her mother's condition, she couldn't possibly go home a few weeks before she was due to give birth to an illegitimate child. So in the end Mummy agreed to go instead.

Mummy had her own reasons for being reluctant to go home. She had divorced without telling her parents, and instead of just the three children they knew about – my elder sisters Marie and Sandra and my brother Michael – she now had my brother Liam as well.

Liam's father, my uncle, was the kind of drunken, irreligious Irishman her mother would probably have crossed the street to avoid. Mummy had never married him, but they were living together, 'in sin' as it was called in those days, which to her Catholic parents would have been worse. On top of it all they were living in a council flat on a run-down estate.

Abandoned

Theirs was a good Catholic family in small-town Ireland, and their parents would never have accepted her lifestyle. Maybe, as her new partner drank more and more, and started to become violent, she was too ashamed to tell *anyone* what her life had come to, let alone her parents. A false pride I can now understand only too well, given how I ended up living years later, too ashamed to bring myself to let anyone know.

With her sister gone to Ireland, Kathy was left to deal with the final two weeks of her pregnancy alone, which no doubt gave her a taste of her own possible future as she struggled to look after her sister's four children in an already cramped, three-bedroom flat. After almost a week, Mummy decided her mother's condition was perhaps not critical, and returned to help Kathy with a pregnancy which, since she couldn't phone to find out, might already have been over. It wasn't, but within days of her sailing home I was born, already six days late, and even on the day of labour in no hurry to arrive. Maybe I realised that it wasn't the greatest ticket to come in on, and needed the extra coaxing: labour began at 2 a.m. and ended just the right side of midnight the following evening.

A few days after my birth another telegram arrived. Again it was from their father, this time even more urgent than the first. Their mother had had a second stroke, almost immediately after Mummy had left Ireland. 'Critical', the telegram said, and this time it didn't leave it to Kathy's conscience to do the right thing – it ordered her home. No excuse on earth would have done.

Mummy rang our 'uncle' Brendan and asked him to go down to her mother and monitor the situation. She arranged for him to call her every night at the same time, on the red telephone box outside the pub where she bought her 'Irish' cigarettes. The reports that came back can't have been good.

Kathy stayed with me as long as she could. I was hastily christened, keeping her surname rather than taking Mummy's married name, the name all the other children in the family had. After all, if Kathy was going to be coming back for me there was no reason for me to have any name but hers. Ten days after I was born she flew home to Ireland to take care of her mother. There was no other option.

I can't imagine what it must have taken for her to do that. What pain she must have been in, before she shut her emotions down, taking care of her mother in that sealed-off world, without a telephone to contact her sister to find out how her baby was doing. Maybe wondering how angry my uncle was at my still being there week after week, and having no one but her married lover to tell her secrets to. Not wanting her mother to die, but knowing too that that was the only way she could go back to get her baby. As her mother's illness worsened – her mind slipping away into dementia, her behaviour more and more childlike by the day – maybe Kathy saw it as some kind of divine retribution, left there washing, dressing and feeding her, nursing her mother instead of the baby she had left behind in England.

As a little girl I heard various versions of what Kathy had planned to do as soon as her mother died or was well enough to leave. In them all she was going to come back to get me. But my grandmother didn't die, though she didn't recover either. Her condition deteriorated and Kathy stayed there looking after her at home for another nine years.

Meanwhile, I grew up in London with my aunt and uncle. And from then on my aunt was the only mother I knew or wanted. And the only one I ever called 'Mummy'. I called my uncle 'Daddy' too, just like my four elder brothers and sisters, and 'the girls' Stella and Jennifer, who came along a few years after I arrived. There were seven of us children in all.

'Don't worry,' Mummy would always whisper after their drunken – often violent – rows, when my uncle would threaten that he wanted me gone by the time he got back from work, 'I won't ever let him send you away, or let anyone come to take you from me.'

'Cross your heart and hope to die?'

'Cross my heart and hope to die.'

Chapter 5

My uncle was a big, well-built Irishman who worked as a labourer on building sites. He came from a large, chaotic family in rural Ireland, and had probably known nothing much more than poverty and abuse in his own childhood. He had small grey eyes, which seemed to follow my every move, and fair hair, which, in the early days, he used to wear almost to his shoulders, with bushy sideburns. He had big, heavy shoulders and hands, and a back full of pimples that he was always getting us to squeeze.

He'd come over to England with three of his brothers to work on the roads, as soon as he'd saved enough for the fare and could legally leave school. Very soon he ended up living a hand-to-mouth existence with Mummy, who was divorced by then with three children of her own and soon pregnant with his first child, my brother Liam. It was a harsh life, which he must have felt completely powerless to change.

It was a struggle just bringing up their own children; another child to feed and clothe can't have been easy. But there were a lot of big families, and poverty and deprivation all around us in the flats at the time, so we weren't really different to the rest.

But the expense of looking after me always came into his tirades against Mummy and me. When she was short he would usually blame her for spending it on me. But he would still refuse to accept any 'hush money' as he called it from Kathy, who as well as caring for her mother had quickly progressed in her career over the years and was relatively comfortably off over in Ireland. Nor would he accept any money from our Uncle Brendan, who in those days was the richest person we knew.

He wanted to get me out – so that they wouldn't keep coming over and interfering in his home – not to be paid to have me there.

It was their visits that really infuriated him. He didn't like anybody from outside coming into his home when we were young, and apart from his brothers we never had any visitors in the flats. When she met him, Mummy had only recently moved down from the North of England, and he knew she had no other family in the country. No one to see what he was doing, or to judge.

But when I was left there all that changed. From then on, to his intense displeasure, both Kathy and our Uncle Brendan would come over and visit us frequently. It must have been a lonely, frightening situation for Mummy before that, knowing no one in London but him, especially when the shine went from their relationship and all the ugliness behind closed doors began.

Mummy was never one to take things lying down. From the stories she told us we knew that even as a child she had been headstrong and unruly, and constantly at war with her own father. She described herself as being the 'black sheep of the family', 'rough and ready' and a 'fighter'.

'Don't worry about me,' she'd whisper to us those nights when we'd all tiptoed back down after he had staggered off to bed. 'I'm as tough as old boots, me.' But she wasn't; though neither was she quite ready for the monster my uncle turned into after swallowing beer and vodka all night. She just wasn't willing to be a victim.

Soon she was fighting fire with fire, matching him vodka for vodka as they tried to scream and pummel one another into the kind of partner they wanted each other to be. Mummy would fight with her last breath to protect her children. And although *she* could say whatever she liked about her own family in Ireland, she saw red whenever my uncle turned on them: especially Kathy. He knew that was the easiest way to get to her, through her red-haired sister with her 'airs and graces' and her distrust of him – Kathy 'the whore'. And so Kathy appeared in our front room like a bad genie out of the vodka bottle every Saturday night, and if that wasn't enough to hurt Mummy, he'd then start on me.

From as early as I can remember hardly a day would pass without my uncle reminding me, in some way or another, that I wasn't a part of that family – that I didn't belong there, and that I wasn't wanted anywhere else either. 'Do you understand?' he'd scream, leaping over to me, the pouf kicked noisily out of the way to intimidate me, or the coffee table upturned, his face turning its purply-red colour in rage.

'Yes, Dad. I'm sorry, Dad,' I'd say, cowering on the settee, my arms covering my head as he punched down on my small body, or my hands clamped over my mouth, trying to stop the crying that would infuriate him even more.

He took his anger out on all of us at times, but even when he was blinded by drink there was still a hierarchy amongst us. His own three children – Liam and 'the girls', Stella and Jennifer – were treated one way, and Mummy's other three children from her earlier marriage – Marie, Sandra and Michael – were treated another way. And then there was me.

But despite the violence and abuse, Mummy stayed with him. 'You make your bed and you lie in it,' was always her philosophy, and he must have shared it because that's what the two of them did.

And so most of my childhood was lived in constant fear. Fear of him and of when he might get Kathy to take me away. It led to me being an insecure, clingy, anxious child, and especially around him I would withdraw into my shell, terrified. But the worse things became, the more I wanted to be there with Mummy and all my brothers and sisters. Like any child I just wanted to fit in and to belong, to be accepted as one of the family I knew as my own. But he seemed just as determined that I never would.

As the years went by I mastered numbness and the near invisibility he demanded, and was almost unreachable by anybody but Mummy. But no matter how good I was, or how useful I became, there was rarely any let-up in his verbal attacks or threats to send me away. There was never a time in all those years when I wasn't terrified of him. And of course the worse he became, the more I dreaded being separated from Mummy.

Abandoned

Even when he was in a good mood, he seemed to enjoy upsetting me. Sometimes, if Mummy had just slipped out on some errand, and one of us noticed and someone asked where she was, he'd say, 'She's not coming back. She's gone for good this time.' He'd be watching me as he said it, amused by the look of shock on my face, nudging one of the boys or winking over at them to make them laugh at my distress. And I would sit rigid until the front door was pushed noisily open and she came back in.

Often, I'd be yelled back out of bed at night during one of their arguments and forced to sit there and listen while his monstrous anger stormed around me and his violent threats to get me out continued. He'd warn me not to cry, but hard as I tried I rarely managed it. Sometimes he'd force me to sit at the oval, smoked-glass table in the dining room to write letters to Kathy telling her I wanted to go over to live with her in Ireland.

The first time I remember it, was not long after one of her visits. Screaming at Mummy through the archway separating the two rooms to go and find paper and envelopes, he made me sit there and write. I can't have been much more than five and could barely write anything without copying out the words. But he made me finish it, hitting me every time I couldn't spell one – my tears, which he screamed at me to stop, turning the words into blue forget-me-nots of ink as they dripped down on to them.

The blood pounded in my ears and my body was stiff with fear while he stood over me, or staggered through the archway between the rooms, shouting out the words, or forcing me to write my own.

> Dear mum
> Please can i come to live with you ~~in Iland~~ there.
> Becwause I want to. you are my mum not mummy and
> i will prefur it there. I am cuming tomorrow on the
> next boat.

Mummy was forced to stay in the front room on the other side of the arch, watching me falling to pieces as I wrote the words that over the years I couldn't bear even to think.

'Don't worry, Anya,' she shouted over him, crying loudly, 'I'll always be your mother. You're going nowhere … I'll never let that be posted. Don't worry about him.'

As I sat there, trying to block out their screams, I was unable to stop trembling. I leaned across the table, squinting to see what I was writing, hot splinters of pain darting beneath my eyelids, my teeth chattering as I willed Mummy to stop arguing back, and myself to stop crying.

'Look at her, look! Look what you're doing to her, you heartless bastard,' she screamed at him.

When I finished I sat tugging down my pink nightdress, trying to control my tears and the pain in my head, waiting for him either to go to bed or to let me go back. I stared down at my pale legs, turned brown under the smoked glass, shrinking them down in my mind to the size of one of the china figures on the mantelpiece, so still and quiet sitting up there that nobody noticed them, hoping my uncle would forget me one day the same way.

Mummy would always refuse to give him Kathy's address in Ireland, and that night she pleaded with him to have a heart, saying it had gone on too long now, that there was nowhere else for me to go, that it would kill her mother if she ever found out Kathy had had a child. He wouldn't listen. While he went off to look for envelopes himself she ran across and tried pulling the letter from me and pushing me out of the chair to get up to bed. But I was paralysed with fear. Tears and mucus streamed down my face as I pushed her away in case he came in and saw her trying to comfort me.

She'd never tell him where the envelopes were either, but he always found them.

'Search all you like, there are none left, you madman,' she screamed, as he stamped around the rooms, slamming drawers in the kitchen, opening and closing cupboards, pulling things out onto the floor. He finally came back with some, throwing the blue airmail envelopes with their stripy red and blue border down with the address book onto the glass and ordering me to find Kathy's address in it and to write it on one.

'I'll get a stamp for that tomorrow … I don't want their left-behinds here, do you hear me?'

I went to bed convinced each time that the letter would be posted and that his threats to send me over to 'them', 'on the next boat', would finally be carried out.

Saturday nights were the worst, the times when the arguments always exploded into violence, him threatening and intimidating and finally lashing out. Sometimes the boys got hit too, but mostly it was me and Mummy.

We were primed by Tom and Jerry earlier in the evening, who showed us that violence was funny. We laughed the cartoon violence off loudly, looking around at each other as we sucked and chewed our way through a bag of pick 'n' mix and slurped our fizzy drinks. Me, the only dark-haired one amongst all my blonde brothers and sisters, trying my hardest to fit in and be invisible to my uncle – trying to put out of my mind the tension I could already feel building between him and Mummy.

But sitting there, waiting for the evening to start, it was hard to shake the pictures of last time still in my head. Pictures I still see now: of Mummy, looking frail and tiny, her small body up against the living room wall; his big, heavy, calloused hands around her throat, the diamond in the gold signet ring on his little finger flashing under the wall-lights as he tightened his grip; her face almost scarlet, her feet lifted off the ground, her eyes bulging, choking. I can still see her collapsing to the ground when he let go; thinking she was dead this time, all the breath gone from my lungs, my heart slamming almost to a stop as I watched her being dragged across the purple carpet by her hair.

She was probably almost as drunk as him by then, kicking and screaming at him to leave us all alone, her skirt up around her hips as he kicked and spat down on her, but still refusing to tell him who my father was. Her voice was tiny and hoarse with emotion and exhaustion but she still defended her sister from being a 'whore' and me from being 'a whore's child'.

I was forced to sit and watch it all after the others had been shouted off to bed. Warned not to cry, pushing my fist or my fingers or my shirt cuffs into my mouth, chewing down on them or the inside of my cheek until my mouth filled with the taste of blood. My shoulders heaving up around my ears, unable to breathe properly as Mummy's screams tore through me. I feel myself slipping away, the room floating in and out, the sounds of her blouse being ripped as he drags her through the archway, shouting that he wants her out too, his knees and fists punching into her as she struggles up and kicks back; vile names I don't yet know the meaning of screamed into both of us. I sit wedged between orange cushions on the end of the fake-leather sofa, shivering, helpless, contorted with fear and the effort to stop my crying, waiting for him to start back on me. The terror of what he is doing and of Mummy leaving forcing my mind out of my body, until the sound of her head being knocked like a coconut against the living room wall jolts me back – not knowing whether to look or not look, listen or not listen, trying to reverse the flow of tears – to stop feeling.

That was the hardest part of growing up: learning not to cry, not even allowed to express the pain of it. Pretending to feel nothing.

Huddling around Mummy after one of the worst fights one night, the TV screen kicked in and glass all over the purple carpet, we planned how we'd get rid of him: a drop of arsenic in his vodka, a sprinkling of rat poison in his stew, a pillow over his face while he slept, or his skull smashed in with one of the girls' heavy, brass lion money-boxes that stood empty either side of the fire surround. We passed one around solemnly, lifting it above our heads, bouncing it up and down on our small, clammy palms, coldly assessing its effectiveness as we demonstrated our love to Mummy through what we were prepared to do.

Abandoned

The solemnity didn't last long. Soon we were laughing away our tears, picking through the evening's violence to find some funny detail to hold on to, to neutralise it, finding some way to release the stored-up emotions, letting them out through tears or laughter. When Mummy joined in, the worst of the pain dissolved, but even though she said he was in a drunken coma in the bedroom by then, I couldn't relax fully; I never could. I always had one eye on the door or, when we eventually moved into a house, on the ceiling, shushing them all if I thought I heard my uncle moving about in his room. My head would be throbbing, my teeth still chattering after his threats to get rid of me again. I would listen out for the creak of floorboards, convinced he would overhear us and come thumping down the stairs two at a time.

The others were frightened of him too, of course. But not always. They were frightened of the drink in him; but when he sobered up they forgot how frightened they were of him when he was drunk and he became their dad again. Sometimes, after the worst of the arguments, he'd come home the next day with a new china ornament to replace the ones he'd smashed, or a brass one to try to win Mummy around, and a bag of pick 'n' mix he'd hand to Stella with orders for her to share them out 'evenly', which included me. Once, after one of the worst arguments, he even brought back a pair of blue budgerigars on a swing in a wire cage. But no matter what, none of the others had to make themselves good enough or invisible enough so that they could stay and belong.

I never had that experience – of thinking he was my dad and trusting him. I was always wary of him. His leaving me alone never lasted long – even when he was sober and trying to get the others back on his side he would ridicule my nervousness around him.

'Shall we kick her out?' he'd say to my brothers and sisters, getting them to join in laughing and teasing me when Mummy was out of the room. I'd sit there swallowing back tears, pretending I didn't care. 'Poor divil,' he'd say.

If Mummy came back in and heard their teasing it often became a trigger for another row. Then I would be seen as the 'troublemaker' again, Liam and Michael whispering under their breaths when they got the chance, 'Why don't you go to live with your *own* mum? You're not wanted here.' Saying it just the way they'd heard my uncle say it all those years.

Chapter 6

Their fights were so loud it was inevitable that the neighbours would sometimes hear. Most people in the flats knew better than to interfere, but occasionally their fights were so bad that people would threaten to call social services and report us. A few times social services did come, but Mummy sent them packing, telling them they had no right to be knocking on her door telling her how to bring up her kids, that we were all well brought up and loved and to check that with the school. It would have been very clear to them that she was a good mother, and if he wasn't there, easy to see how they would leave us alone.

One morning, though, Mummy told me a man was coming to talk to us, just me and her, and I got to come home early from school, before the others. I sat on the settee in my best summer dress and new white socks while he and Mummy talked. What they talked about was me, and I listened closely. He was a tall, thin man in a tight brown suit who must have been about the same age as my uncle at the time, in his mid-thirties. He appeared too tall to sit on our settee, perching awkwardly on the edge with his brown leather briefcase on his lap; his back shaped into a letter 'C' as he bent over it and his knees up almost to his chin. He said no to the tea and the eight custard creams

Mummy had laid out on one of the blue plates for him, and turned down cigarettes too, dismissing them without looking up, with a wave of a long, hairy hand that was all loose-boned, like a skeleton's.

He clicked the briefcase open and took out a large notebook and a blue folder of papers. I strained to see what was written on them, but Mummy caught my eye and shook her head. Mummy had told me he was going to be asking lots of questions and that if he asked if I liked my uncle to just say yes.

Every question seemed like a trap. He asked me what the names of all my brothers and sisters were, and which one was my favourite, and did I mind having a different surname to them, and did I like school and what was my favourite lesson? When he suddenly smiled and asked who I liked best, Mummy or Daddy, I said Mummy, and then quickly changed it to a shrug, worried that he might send me to Ireland to live with Kathy if I didn't. I sat there nervously, wiping my hot hands on the cushions. But I felt special sitting there too, in my best clothes and in all the peace and quiet, without all my brothers and sisters talking over me.

Whenever he bent to write answers in his book, mine and Mummy's eyes glanced at each other across the room swiftly, then away again, like birds flying to and fro across the sky. Mummy was small and pale and the only one in the family with dark hair like me, and I loved it when people said, 'Don't you look like your mum?' or to Mummy, 'Doesn't she look like you?' Sometimes Mummy ruffled my hair and smiled down at me saying nothing, but other times she said almost proudly, 'She's my sister's little one.'

Abandoned

As I sat there, I thought of the way she sometimes said that, trying to shuffle it all straight in my head again, telling myself I didn't care because Mummy was my real mum really. I looked over at her staring back at me. Her face looked sad and thin and her head was shaking in a way that frightened me. I felt my eyes well up with tears at all the trouble I was causing.

Next time he scribbled something, without moving her head Mummy curled her lip over her top teeth and did buckteeth, pointing at him, and I had to press my fingers over my mouth to stop myself from laughing. She shook her head and pulled a serious face to tell me not to, and I sat on my hands to stop myself from feeling anything at all, trying not to think of his buckteeth. I tried to do everything right and to sit still, and at the end I think we 'passed' because he shook Mummy's hand when he left and patted me on the head.

After he'd gone Mummy looked tired and smoked a lot. I swivelled my eyes over to the biscuits still on the plate.

'Looking down his nose at us,' she sniffed. 'At least I have the manners to accept a cup of tea and a biscuit when it's offered to me.'

Mummy looked sad and I felt shivery, wondering if it was anything to do with me. In my head I saw the man's buckteeth again and looked at the hard cream sandwiched between the biscuits. I thought of Mummy doing the buckteeth earlier to make me smile.

'Maybe he only eats carrots,' I said shyly.

I felt Mummy's smile before I saw it, and looked up at her as it grew longer and longer, spreading across her face until she was laughing and tears were rolling down her cheeks. Suddenly she found the energy to get up, ruffling my hair as she passed into the kitchen, saying I was a great girl, and that nobody was taking me away from her, and I could have all the custard creams 'quick, before the others come in'.

I bit into one, stuffing the rest into the front pockets of my dress, glad that nobody else was here, just me and Mummy and the whole place warm and quiet, all to ourselves, with the gas fire on and the clock ticking quietly up on the wall and everything put away, and the smell of polish everywhere. When I looked up at Mummy I could see that the tears had rinsed all the pain from her eyes, and when she smiled back at me, her blue eyes shining into mine, the smile spread all through me. Custard creams were the best taste in the world after that.

Chapter 7

The man my uncle thought was most likely to be my father, and who I secretly wished was, was also the type of man he despised: an Irishman who was the opposite in almost every way to him. He was a colleague of Kathy's, someone who frequently came over from Ireland on business to meet clients and so could visit us more often than her. He never stayed with us when he came over, as Kathy always did. Instead he would stay in 'posh' hotels and visit us in black taxis or shiny rented cars, usually while my uncle was at work. Just the mention of his name sent my uncle into a rage.

We came to know him as our rich, kind Uncle Brendan, who never hit anyone or raised his voice and who always smiled and tried to get me to talk. He was the only man any of us ever knew, except for our headmaster, who wore a shirt and tie and shoes you could see your face in, every day of the week, not just to dress up to go to the pub in on a Saturday night. He was definitely the only man, Irish or otherwise, any of us knew who didn't drink.

He always singled me out for special attention because he was Kathy's friend and the only person in Ireland who knew about my existence. My brothers and sisters were bemused after my uncle's treatment of me as to why anyone should pay me any attention at all. By coming to visit us, he was 'doing Kathy a favour', Mummy said. But my uncle didn't want any 'favours' from anyone, especially him.

Without the others knowing, I would be put into taxis to visit him at one of the big hotels in central London where he met his clients. I would tap hesitantly in new shoes across the vast marble lobbies, past displays of flowers almost as big as myself fanned out on antique tables, and into quiet hotel restaurants filled with gilt mirrors, silver candelabra and stiff, white tablecloths. It was all a world away from where we lived in the flats.

Brendan seemed fascinated by my shyness. It seemed to put him at his ease too, and when we were alone together he went out of his way to try to put me at mine. He always seemed more relaxed when there were no grown-ups about. He talked more and seemed to relish the opportunity to come down to a child's level. He drank glasses of Coca-Cola through straws in glasses clinking with ice and, declining the heavy, leather menus, would order cheeseburgers and knickerbocker glories, or steaks full of blood and plates piled high with profiteroles. I blushed at the smiling waiters and at Brendan's questions about things at home, and tried not to wonder how Mummy and I would pay for this when my uncle found out where I'd been all day. But especially with who.

Sometimes I would stay a night or two with him at whichever hotel he was staying at. I always got picked on for this by my brothers and sisters when I got back, and wished Brendan would treat us all the same, but he never did. When he visited the flats he'd take me to Mass at the local Catholic church with him too. Although all of us had

been christened, we never went to church, so it was a
novelty when Brendan visited. God was another secret
too, something I could only talk about with Mummy. I
wasn't allowed to tell any of my brothers and sisters in
case they told my uncle. He'd go mad if he knew Brendan
was taking me to church.

Behind their backs he already called both Kathy and
Brendan 'hypocrites' and 'Holy Joes' and warned my brothers and sisters that they weren't allowed to go anywhere
near a church with them. So it was a special time, just me
and him. He taught me when to sit and stand or kneel, and
when to clasp my hands in prayer, knotting my fingers
together like he did. Though on one visit he terrified me by
telling me about the Holy Spirit prowling invisibly up and
down the aisle reading everybody's thoughts; swooping
down, when you least expected it, on anyone with bad ones.
After that I feared the Holy Spirit, who could see inside
everyone's minds as Brendan said, certain that he must
know the bad thoughts I had about my uncle.

Brendan didn't know most of what my uncle did at
home – how drunk he got and how violent he was to me
and Mummy. Before their visits Mummy made me promise
not to tell him or Kathy about the rows and his threats.
'Nosy parkers,' she'd say, striking a match to another cigarette and wrestling a smile out of me as she blew it out
noisily. 'It's none of their business what goes on in our
home, is it?'

I would shake my head loyally, but was always unable to
look directly up at her, wondering why she didn't want
them to know so that they could help us.

* * *

Either Kathy or Brendan came over every few months, apparently unaware of the disruption they were causing in our home. Their visits felt like charades. Everyone on their best behaviour, my brothers and sisters leaving me be, my uncle biting his tongue – his long, aggressive silences scaring me just as much as the eruptions of anger I came to expect the minute they'd gone.

Kathy always dressed exquisitely: silk blouses with high, queenly collars, and cuffs with small pearl buttons, elegant and feminine, her perfume clinging to everything. Brendan would be dressed as usual in his suit and tie, sitting awkwardly in the living room, his cup of tea balanced on his thigh, snapping biscuits and brushing away the crumbs as he tried to make small talk over my uncle's hostility and laughed anxiously at anything at all; a teetotaller and a near alcoholic eyeing each other across the room. Looking back now, I can understand that my uncle was furious at being made a fool of in his own home. But as a child I had no such understanding.

I dreaded Kathy's visits because everyone was always reminding me that she was my real mother, and because up to the moment of them my uncle would usually be threatening that this time he would see to it that she would take me away with her. I convinced myself that I hated her because my uncle said she was a 'whore', and Mummy got into such trouble for me being left there. And because Mummy couldn't look like her or spend all her time doing her hair and make-up or walk around in high, clicky heels, when she was 'working her fingers to the bone' for all of us.

Mostly I made myself hate her because I already had my mum and my family and I didn't want another one. I just wanted everyone to forget that she was the one who had given birth to me, and for her to go away and leave us alone. I wanted to belong where I was.

Sometimes, though, I would forget to hate Kathy. Her soft, smiling, gentle Irishness would sneak up on me and I would feel tricked when I caught myself liking her. I always had to keep my guard up.

Before her visits, my brothers and sisters led by my uncle would mimic and ridicule her: the way she walked and talked; her gentleness and dainty 'put on' manners, as my uncle called them. I laughed shyly along with everyone else, always trying to fit in, to be accepted. I thought that if my uncle could see how much I hated her, then maybe he wouldn't say those things about me any more, and would let me belong there with the rest of them. But although I played along, I couldn't stop the defensive feelings that flared up inside me when the others laughed about her. And I couldn't stop thinking about her in secret even though it felt like I was being disloyal to Mummy.

It was when I saw Mummy getting hit and shouted at for defending her sister that it was easiest to hate Kathy. And when I listened to Mummy sobbing later, after the arguments, looking pale and tired and suddenly very small, slumped on her corner of the sofa with her purple dressing gown zipped up to the chin and the cushions wedged around her like sandbags, I hated her most. I would watch helplessly as Mummy tore off sheets of toilet paper from a roll and cried into them, blaming her sister for dumping her problems on her, and for the easy life she had 'swanning about the place', living 'a life of luxury', while Mummy was left looking after us lot with no time even to look at her nails, 'let alone paint them'.

Abandoned

'Doing her dirty work for her,' was my uncle's term for looking after me, and Mummy sometimes used the same words herself when she'd drunk too much. That was when I was most determined not to like Kathy, no matter how soft and gentle she was, or how nice she was to me. I'd sit next to Mummy, frowning it all into place, my heart being squeezed tight, hate for Kathy rushing down to my toes.

They were not feelings that simply disappeared when Kathy came over, and I never understood how Mummy could forget it all and be best friends with her on her next visit. Despite my feelings, and Daddy's threats the night before, I would get carried along in all the excitement before she arrived, and would run down to the square in front of our block with the others to carry up her bags and suitcases from the black taxi. We would all struggle like little Sherpas up the steps to the second floor, wondering how much of the weight was presents and sweets and which bags they were in, huffing and puffing along the landing, wondering what lotions and creams were in the blue, leather vanity case that Stella always carried up. But I was still upset for Mummy.

Later, after some of the bags were opened and presents unwrapped, Mummy and Kathy would go out together to the shops or just for a stroll. I would crouch down to watch through the small iron grille in the red brick wall of the landing as Mummy linked her arm through Kathy's fur-covered one and walked her the long way around the estate to the shops, showing her sister off, holding on to her as if she were some lucky charm, our family shamrock.

Kathy often had tears in her eyes before they went out for those strolls, or when she first got out of the taxi and saw us all standing there in our best clothes smiling up at her, her big, navy-blue eyes welling up with tears. Her tears fascinated me but I never trusted them; they seemed too gentle, too delicate. She didn't sob and howl like Mummy did; she didn't rip your heart out.

Chapter 8

My older sisters, Marie and Sandra, were almost a different generation to us five younger ones. They were teenagers when we were still very little.

Of us three younger girls I was the eldest. Stella was two and a half years younger than me and my uncle's real daughter. She was born premature – sick and tiny, small as the palm of your hand, Mummy said – and at first she slept in an empty drawer at the side of their bed. My uncle adored her from the start. Even when he was drunk, she was the only one able to bring out his softer side. Mummy often shouted at him, saying he was giving her attention on purpose to try to make me feel even more left out.

When she was born he found a use for me. I had to look after her. I was told never to let her out of my sight, and had to go with her wherever she went. As she grew older he told her that if I didn't do everything she said, or did anything wrong, she had to tell him when he came back from work, and she would, even though Mummy would warn her not to, or even if I pleaded with her. She was *his* favourite, not Mummy's, and also his pawn.

'I don't care,' she'd say defiantly. 'I'm telling.'

Mummy called her a traitor, and told me not to worry, that she'd treat me the next day when my uncle wasn't there. But Stella didn't care, running across the square to meet him from work some evenings. I watched her long blonde hair swinging across her back as she skipped off, like a canary sent ahead down a mine. If he was in a bad mood she'd return on her own and sit in front of the TV with her face screwed up, and I would wait, trembling. If she reappeared around the corner swinging off his arm it wasn't as bad, although I never knew what she had told him.

Sometimes, she wouldn't tell him immediately. She would draw the agony out all evening. I would sit on the end of the settee, like one of the statues on the mantelpiece, waiting to be smashed. Just when I was starting to think she'd forgotten, as we all sat squashed up together on the settee, she would stretch up with a little yawn in her pink nightdress and say out of the blue, 'Someone did something today.'

'Did what?' he'd ask, and she'd tell whatever it was.

'Broke a cup,' she'd say, without taking her eyes from the TV, and my heart would stop.

'Who?' my uncle would ask, while Mummy swung around to Stella with a tight, angry face that said 'You wait, you little troublemaker.'

'Good girl, Stella, you tell me what they've been up to,' he would say as Mummy scowled at her. And he would take another opportunity to punish me.

Sometimes, if he was in a good mood, she'd get up onto his lap and fall asleep there, curled up like a kitten. But as soon as she felt ready she would say, 'Come on, Anya, I want to go to bed.' Even if it was near the end of the programme we were watching, just when we were about to find out what happened, I had to go with her. Mummy would try to make her wait, or tell her to go on her own.

'She's old enough to go on her own now,' she'd say, if my uncle was in the right mood.

'No, I want Anya to come,' Stella would insist.

I couldn't say anything in front of my uncle, and she knew it. So I would have to lie in bed thinking about the programme the others were still watching, trying to guess what happened next.

When my uncle couldn't stand the sight of me any longer he would send me out to the kitchen to stand in the dark. In our small flat there was nowhere else to send me.

'She'll stay there until her whore of a mother gets here to take her back over with her,' he'd say.

He used to send Marie and Sandra out to the kitchen too. But they were older by then and had to clean while they were there. He'd send one of us out to check up on what they were doing.

'Sneak up on them,' he'd say, trying to get us all not trusting each other. 'Don't talk to them, just check and then come back and tell me what they're doing, d'you hear?'

If we didn't tell the truth, or warned them that he had sent us out, we were the ones that got hit. He always seemed to know.

Sometimes, if they were both out there together for some reason, he'd make us stand outside the door to hear what they were talking about. He always thought everyone was whispering about him. Mummy said he was 'paranoid'. 'Sick in the head with all the drink, you are,' she'd shout at him, as he shut the door on her and tiptoed along the hallway to see what one of us was doing, or saying about him.

Abandoned

When he first sent me out to the kitchen I was too young to clean it. I just had to stand in the dark. I wasn't allowed to sit or turn on the light or move from the exact spot on the red lino where he'd told me to stand. The kitchen was always cold and if he'd thrown me out there in the middle of one of their rows, I'd be there for hours, until Mummy fought for me to come back in, or to be allowed to go to bed with the others when it was time.

I didn't mind it in the kitchen most times. It was quiet and the short, red checked curtains were so thin that even with them drawn I could see from the landing light outside. I would read the backs of boxes and jars of food, finding things to do: a box of Cornflakes weighs 225g, divide by 2 that's? Add 7? Minus 15? Times 5? I practised school work: doing sums, memorising the spellings on the packaging and telling stories inside my head. If I got all the spellings right I would lick my finger and have a dip in the sugar bowl, smiling at how naughty I was being. Inside my head I'd say, 'I don't care,' and pull my nightie off one shoulder and shrug it bare like Stella did to make my uncle laugh. It felt as if I'd got a friend there that I was talking to.

Sometimes when I was sent to the kitchen Mummy would decide she'd had enough. Instead of whispering in to me when she came past to go to the toilet that she would 'treat me tomorrow', she would come barging out, saying, 'No … no, I'm not having this,' and switch on the light, talking in a loud voice and then whispering down to me, 'It's alright, it'll give him a fright.' She'd then return to her screaming voice, calling him names and trying to drag me back in behind her, my heart tumbling about in my chest as I tried to resist and grab things to hold on to, trying to stay where he told me.

Abandoned

Occasionally she would win. But most times he jumped up and was there behind her, forcing me to get back, and Mummy would get hit instead. When she shouted louder than him and managed to pull me back into the front room, she would push me onto the end of the settee, telling the others to move up and to make room for me.

'She's staying there, right? I'm not having her treated any different to the others.'

But he never stopped threatening things. Even if he had slept off his rage and woken up quiet, I wasn't allowed to move on the settee or make a sound. Even if someone pinched me to move up I couldn't pinch back, not while he was there.

Soon the settee wasn't big enough for five of us and one of us sometimes had to sit on the floor. I loved being up on the settee, squashed in amongst the others, but if my uncle was in a good mood Stella might say, 'I'm too hot, sit on the floor, Anya.' And my uncle would laugh with her and I'd have to sit on the floor.

'No, she won't,' Mummy would say to Stella. 'You sit on the floor, madam, and just shut up – I'm warning you.'

I wished Mummy would let me fight my own battles. I was willing to sit on the floor if it meant I could have some peace.

The others used to sit like statues in a row on the settee and refuse to look at me after fights, after he'd told them not to talk to me, that I wasn't one of them. I knew they hated me for all the trouble I caused by being there, and for making them take sides when Mummy and their dad argued. I know they thought it was my fault. Me the trou-blemaker again.

Later, in bed, I'd burrow down into last night's wet sheets and lie there crying, trying to find a way to stop the tears and everyone picking on me. But when I woke up in wet sheets again the next morning they'd start up again. It would be years before I stopped wetting the bed most nights.

If he woke up in his armchair and heard us whispering around him, trying not to wake him, he would fly into one of his rages and his mantra would start up again. 'She's out,' he'd shout again, meaning me, his hand flying out, and the gold signet ring on his little finger busting my lip.

'Don't listen to him, okay,' Mummy would say to me after the rows, when she came out to the kitchen to check I was okay. When I asked her what I'd done wrong and what I had to do so that I wasn't in the way, like he said I was, she would pull me to her, ruffling my hair, telling me I was never in the way.

'Don't mind him. You're as good as gold, better than all the rest of them put together,' she'd say.

I was always frightened he would come in and catch her talking to me, but she would refuse to go back into the front room until I'd given her a smile. She'd lift my face to look at her and stick her tongue out, pulling funny faces and flicking V-signs towards him in the dark, until eventu-ally she made me smile.

'One day me and you are going to leave this place, okay?' she'd say, lifting my chin and trying to make me look into her eyes. 'Just you and me, okay.'

Abandoned

I probably believed her the first few times. I stopped believing everything after a while.

When everyone was at home, there were nine of us, including Mummy and my uncle, so you could never be on your own unless you were being punished. In a way I liked it when I was sent outside and all the sound stopped and I could think of things, or of nothing at all. For a while he used to send me to the bedroom the five of us younger ones shared, and it was nice because I could read. Although once, when I lay on the bed happily reading a book, chewing a Black Jack I'd found in the lining of Sandra's jacket, he caught me and laid into me, tearing the book away and ripping out its pages. From then on, when I was sent there I had to keep the lights off. But if one of the others tipped me off that he'd gone to sleep in his armchair I would sometimes risk standing on the bed and go under the curtains to read on the windowsill by the bright light on the landing outside our flat, escaping into the better worlds in stories.

Chapter 9

Liam blamed me for everything. He was only eight months older than me, but when I came along he had to share Mummy with me. He grew up listening to my uncle shout at me, and copied him, picking on me, accusing me of being a troublemaker and of being in the way.

I hated the spiteful way he would tell me I wasn't wanted, that I should go back to my *own* mum, with his skinny little chest stuck out and his shoulders back, sounding like he really meant it, just like my uncle. But sometimes he was just quiet and let me be his sister, and as long as Mummy didn't make it worse by shouting at him to leave me alone I could stand up to him for myself.

Liam was the one I looked up to the most, the one I most wanted to be friends with. He was my uncle's real son and, like Stella and Jennifer, was treated differently. I knew instinctively that if I could get him to stop teasing me and to like me then the others would too. They were all just copying him, just like he was copying my uncle.

Liam, Michael, Stella, Jennifer and I all went to the local school, which was on the edge of the estate, a few minutes' walk away from our block. I tried to keep my head down at school and not draw any attention to myself, to cover up what went on at home. I was quiet and bookish and in many ways an easy target for bullies. But whatever the bullies did was never as bad as what my uncle did to me. School was a sanctuary from home, and no matter how bad it got it was always bearable.

In the playground one day, some of the bullies in my class found out I'd got four brothers and sisters in the school. They hadn't realised before because of my different surname, and it felt good. Having them know I was one of five, instead of on my own, made me feel safe. Even though they didn't know who my brothers and sisters were, it seemed to make me more popular for a while. They stopped picking on me, and I wasn't always the last to be chosen for games. Then, one lunchtime, they said they didn't believe me, and a group of them walked me around the playground, making me pick my brothers and sisters out, one by one.

I pointed out the two small, blonde girls in the infants' playground, swinging and jumping with the others, then the two bigger boys, playing separately, each in their own gang.

'See,' I said. It made me feel warm all over that everyone knew I had them there.

'Why are they all blonde and you've got that dirty gravy-coloured hair?' one girl from another class asked.

'I don't care,' I replied, which was a response I was trying to teach myself to feel at home.

For the next few days there was a wide, safe space around me in class, no one getting close enough to push me or tell me I smelt, or make fun of the hand-me-down clothes of Sandra's I wore, or the old-fashioned boots which someone gave Mummy and which she made me wear to school when it rained. But the bullies grew impatient after a while.

'You're lying,' the biggest of them accused me before class one day. 'They're not your brothers and sisters.'

For a minute it sounded like my uncle saying it, and I could almost hear Mummy shouting back, 'Yes they are, you cruel bastard, leave her alone.'

'Yes, they are,' I said.

'*None* of them are your brothers or sisters,' she spat.

I wanted to shout again that they were, but nothing came out, and I just nodded and nodded without stopping, as the spiky laughter went on around me, until the teacher came in, smiling, and saw me nodding.

'Yes, what?' she said.

They all turned and started laughing again. When I lifted my head to look at the teacher for support she looked away quickly, as if my face had frightened her, and started writing the date in yellow chalk in the corner of the blackboard.

They carried on at lunch break, surrounding me. 'Why have you got a different surname then?'

I didn't know how to explain that although I had a different surname to the others I was the one who was 'never going to be sent away'. I just shrugged.

'Names don't matter.'

Mummy always said it was the 'inside things' that mattered, what you feel on the inside, and so they *were* my real brothers and sisters, and they always would be.

'They can't be your brothers and sisters if you've got different surnames,' my tormentor said again. I just walked away fast, humming. Nothing was going to stop me believing it. They *were* my brothers and sisters.

Abandoned

'Why didn't your *own* mum want you?' they asked for a few days after that, crowding around me, breathing up all the air. Their words hit home. I felt a cold, heavy, sick sensation slip down inside me.

'She does want me. I've got my mum, she's indoors,' I said, slamming my hands over my ears and running off fast.

But they ran after me through the playground shouting, 'She's not your mum, she's not your mum, you dirty skinny liar!'

Even when the bell went and we had to get in line to go in, my heart wouldn't stop pounding. It punched and punched against my ribcage, as if it had had enough and wanted to escape. And when Miss stood at the board and talked about how to do paragraphs, it was still so noisy that I thought she was about to spin around and tell me to 'stop that racket', that she couldn't hear herself think. I leaned forwards until the edge of the desk was digging into my stomach, and my heart-noise quietened to a steady bom-bom, bom-bom, like one of the slow trains climbing up the hill behind the shops.

Our block was directly opposite the school, across a narrow one-way road. Because it wasn't a main road Mummy didn't have to collect us; we all just met up at the top gate and ran across. Liam had the key to get in on a piece of green string around his neck. Most of the children in my class lived at the other end of the school, and used the other gate where their mums queued up to collect them with sweets and crisps, so they didn't see us all going home together.

Abandoned

One day the top gate was still padlocked so we had to use the bottom one. Liam and I were there first and we had to stand around and wait for the others. The two girls from my class with the lightest blonde hair marched up to Liam.

'Is your mum her mum?'

It was the wrong time to ask him. He was in a temper with me, standing by the boys' toilets, furiously scraping the cement out between bricks with the point of a compass. It was the kind of time when he might say anything. My heart stopped and I stared at him without blinking, crossing my fingers inside my anorak pocket. But straight away he said, 'No.'

'Yes, she is,' I said to all of them, almost before he had got the word out, but four bright-blue eyes were glaring between mine and Liam's, and I knew they believed him, not me.

'So she's not your sister, then?'

Liam was in the year above, and bigger than all of them. Not afraid of anyone either, just like my uncle. 'I just told you, didn't I? Are you deaf? Or just plain stupid?'

He said it exactly the way my uncle would, and it made me look up at him again, at his tight face, pale and narrow; his little pink scar from where my uncle had thrown the bread knife at Mummy and missed, raised like a trophy on his forehead; the throb high up in the muscles of his jaw going just like my uncle's went before he snapped. I was in awe of his ability to answer back the bullies. He wouldn't look at me, just stared at a point in the distance, his eyes grey and unblinking, those same little chips of concrete as my uncle's.

'Liar.' The girls turned on me, their faces vicious. I swung my head back towards Liam, wanting him to give them one of his punches, or twist their arms in a Chinese burn.

I shrugged. 'Sticks and stones may break my bones but names will never hurt me,' I heard Mummy singing in my head as I walked away.

But things were going to get much worse than just shouting and cruel words.

Chapter 10

The idea of me going away to boarding school had started with Kathy bringing some brochures over in her suitcase. One afternoon, not long after that, Marie leaned over the balcony and called me up from the square. She was seventeen by then, one of the grown-ups as far as we were concerned. It wasn't raining, so I knew we were not all being called in because of that, and she only wanted me. I heard the slap of Stella's skipping rope slow to a stop behind me and she ran over.

'What do you want Anya for?'

'I've just got a small job for her,' Marie said, 'that's all. Stay down there, she won't be long.'

Stella complained and started, 'Daddy said ...' which made my heart thump. We all knew what my uncle said I had to do; I had to stay with Stella, and do whatever she wanted me to do. But this time Marie cut her off.

'She won't be a minute, okay,' she said in a firm voice, calling me on with her finger. As I walked up I could feel Stella's anger behind me.

'You wait till Daddy gets home,' she shouted after me. 'I'm telling.'

My uncle would go mad that I'd defied her. All the way up the stairs and across the landing my heart was thumping.

Marie took me into her bedroom. Over my shoulder as I looked back from the doorway I could see Mummy in the bright kitchen, peeling potatoes; her hair scraped back, her face tired and lumpy. Her eyes were rimmed with red and her face stained with tears. Something was wrong. Why didn't she look up at us? The bedroom door clicked shut behind us and I tried to swallow quietly. It felt strange sitting on the bed with Marie. I felt the cold I brought up with me clinging to my jumper, and when Marie smiled at me and started to talk I felt my mouth smile back, but the rest of me checked the door and the windows and thought about Mummy in the kitchen with her strained face and red eyes.

Marie went on talking to me in a sleepy kind of voice about how grown-up I was getting, and how bad my uncle could be, and how it was nothing to do with me, and did I know that? I nodded that I did, not sure if that was a black lie or a white one, and crossed my fingers in my pocket just in case. But at the back of my head I was still seeing Mummy with all the potato peelings in the colander and her red eyes, and Stella standing in the stairwell yelling, 'I'm telling,' wanting me to go back down and play games that I was two years too old for.

I banged my legs back quietly against the side of the bed and stared at a bottle of pink nail varnish Kathy had left behind last time she visited, sitting on the big, curvy, brown dressing table. I wondered what Marie was saying all this for, and why we were here while Mummy was in the other room with red eyes.

'It's not nice to be sad, is it?' Marie said. 'The boys are horrible sometimes, aren't they?' I nodded again, looking down at my grazed knee, twisting the hem of my jumper around my fingers, wondering if this was a trick, even when she said 'I think so too.'

Then it came; she told me about schools where girls go to sleep and come back for holidays. But it didn't mean they were bad and had been sent away, she said. I stopped banging my legs and froze. Before she finished I was already crying and shaking my head and saying I didn't want to go. She told me it would be a really 'lucky' place to go, and that my uncle wouldn't pick on me or hit me there, and neither would anyone else, and that I could still come back to live with Mummy in the holidays.

She tried to make me look at some of the brochures she'd taken down from a hiding place on top of the wardrobe. I watched all the furry grey dust falling down with them. I was never disobedient, but I shook my head and folded my arms so she couldn't make me hold them. She put them down on the pillow instead.

'Does Mummy want me to go?' I asked.

'Only if you want to.'

'I don't,' I said, barely taking a breath in between, and looked straight back at her big blue eyes. 'I've got my own school.'

She talked more, saying it wasn't like I thought, that I wasn't getting sent away because Mummy didn't want me there, but that Kathy had offered to pay for it, and she and Mummy thought it would be good for me. I shut her voice out, the way I did when the others said Mummy was not my real mum. She asked if I would at least think about it while she went to the toilet, and I shook my head again, kicking my legs harder against the bed.

'Just think about it,' she said, 'please, for Mummy.'

Abandoned

I shrugged and she said to just look at the pictures, please would I, and it was all up to me, I could choose whichever one of the schools I liked to go to, and if I didn't like it when I got there I could come right back. She promised, on 'Mummy's life', but she knew I'd like it, she said. 'You'll have lots of friends of your own age.'

Marie clicked the door closed behind her as she went out, and I picked my scab, listening to the voices of everyone playing in the square downstairs, all my friends. Through the wall I heard Marie and Mummy talking in the kitchen in low voices, as if my uncle was back. I held my breath and listened harder through the thumping of my heart, and when I was sure he wasn't there I tried to make my breathing smooth again.

I tried not to see the glossy white brochures she'd left on the pillow, but there was no one there to see me. Clicking my tongue against the roof of my mouth nervously, I opened the top brochure and looked at the pictures of girls in pleated skirts running in playing fields, carrying sticks with little nets on the end; and sitting at desks, wearing stripy dresses with short sleeves, reading books; and another one of them wearing long white overalls and big plastic glasses, standing at wooden benches in front of metal candles with bright flames. Everyone was laughing or smiling, and I could tell there were no boys around, shouting. But I remembered the brochures had come from Kathy, which gave me another reason for hating these places.

When I heard the toilet flush I quickly closed the top page and sat up straight, trying to slow my breathing. The door clicked open and Marie asked if I'd thought about it. I nodded.

'What do you think?'

'I think I'm not going. Can I go back downstairs to look after Stella now?'

She let me go and my eyes clashed with Mummy's on the way out. I could see she'd been crying more but Marie put her hand on my shoulder and steered me past, without letting me talk to her. I ran along the landing, frowning, trying to loosen the tight feeling in my belly. Marie was out, leaning over the balcony by the time I got down, and I called up.

'Did you tell Mummy I didn't even look at the pictures?'

'Not yet,' she said in a tired voice.

'Tell her, don't forget … Say, "She didn't even look at one picture."'

I ran off proudly, happy that Mummy knew I wanted to stay with her and not go away to live in Ireland or to a 'sleeping-school'. I could feel Marie watching me from the balcony. There was always someone staring at me these days: Brendan standing outside the school railings looking in at me as I sat reading on the steps in the playground; or Kathy staring in at us through the gap in the half-opened bedroom door as we all lay on the carpet doing the jigsaw puzzles she'd brought us; or looking up in class and seeing Miss's shaky smile when I stared at her; everyone suddenly looking at me as if I'd done something wrong.

I didn't need friends in school anyway. I had lots of brothers and sisters when I came home, and they were enough. People outside our home were 'nosy parkers', and I didn't tell anyone our business. I knew Marie thought I didn't have any friends anywhere and that was why I should go away to a sleeping-school, but there were loads of children to play with in the flats. I looked up over my shoulder and saw that Mummy was out with Marie on the landing now too. They were turned towards one another talking, with their arms folded up on the landing wall. I watched Mummy's cigarette smoke stream into Marie's long blonde hair and thought she was probably telling her that I wasn't in the way and that she didn't want me to go anywhere, and that I'd got my own bed to sleep in and didn't need to go away to a school to sleep.

In case she looked down I skipped across the square, humming loudly to show her I wasn't sad on my own. I hoped they weren't looking down at me, both thinking that I didn't belong there. I ran over to the bigger girls at the skipping rope queue and stood at the end, looking up at the balcony to see if they were still there watching.

Jackie, from one of the flats on the top floor, said the rope was too high for me, but I refused to go away and said, 'I don't care. I know I can jump it this time. I'm playing anyway.'

They laughed at me and let me stay and I beamed up at Mummy and Marie, pressing closer to the girl in front of me so they knew she was my friend, singing the skipping rope songs as loudly as I could, with a hot feeling in my tummy. Marie and Mummy waved back, and Mummy's smile told me that she knew I'd got my own friends and that I belonged right there with her.

Nobody mentioned the school for a while after that. But whenever Mummy stopped to have a cigarette or to sit down with a cup of tea, I saw her face about to talk about it and I would get up and do something to make myself useful.

'Do you want me to help you clean the drawers out?' I would volunteer. 'I'll make the beds. I can make them on my own now.'

Abandoned

'I don't know what I'd do without you,' she'd say. 'You're better than all the rest of them put together.'

I had no idea Marie had been offering me an escape route or how much worse things were about to get.

Chapter 11

I've woken up too early. The light in the bedroom is the colour of fish tank water, and my eyes swim up drowsily through it towards the sounds in the middle of the room. It's my first morning waking up in the 'big girls' bedroom that Marie and Sandra share by the front door, and everything is unfamiliar. I'm supposed to be getting up early to go with Marie to the train station. I have to bring the child benefit money back from the post office, hiding it in my sock and crossing two main roads and then the streets with the trees and big houses, and then the footbridge back to the flats on my own. I've never done that before and Mummy's worried that I'm too young. But she is on a new shift and has to go into work early, before we all get up, and Michael needs money for a school trip. There's no other way to do it, and so in the end she agrees. I'm not yet seven and excited at the thought of proving how useful I can be, but even more excited at sleeping in the 'big girls' room and soon being one of them, no longer having to sleep in the back room with all the younger ones.

The noises sound like voices, whispers, and I wonder if Marie has forgotten about me. I push back the blankets and sit up on my knees, shivering, hugging myself against the cold as I blink into the thick, green light, trying to remember which end of the room the bed is. The big double wardrobe, with its rusty key hanging from a piece of red string, comes bulging out of the dark and I run my eyes across the crack of yellow light under the door to the hallway, and then back around the room.

Then I see Marie with her back to me. She has her white work shirt on and her blonde hair is hanging loose down her back, almost to her waist. She has no skirt on. I'm about to ask her if it's time to wake up, but then the dark dissolves a bit more and when she moves her shoulder I see that my uncle is there, standing up against her. I freeze. Suddenly everything is wrong. *My uncle never goes into the bedrooms.* He has his arms around her waist and is kissing her. It doesn't make sense. I lean forwards, frowning, and the coats that covered the bed during the night fall heavily onto the floor. Instinctively I try to hide back under the covers but it's too late; my uncle looks over Marie's shoulder and sees me.

He pushes Marie out of the way and comes hurtling towards me, shouting, the buckle on his open belt clattering, his fists thumping me down into the bed, then dragging me out by the hair, throwing me across the floor as if I'm a sack of concrete he's pulling from the back of a trailer, instead of a stunned six-year-old in stripy blue pyjamas.

My arms are clamped over my head and his big, heavy hands are dragging and slamming me as I cry, 'Sorry, Dad ... sorry,' looking up at his livid face, the dark rope of muscles at the side of his throat jumping like eels. But I'm not sure what I am saying sorry about. Why was he kissing her in the middle of the bedroom? Nobody kisses *anybody* in our home. Marie and my uncle are screaming over me, and behind them I see the boys in their vests and underpants, standing in the hallway watching.

'Get her out of here. What's she doing here? The sly bitch,' he shouts, kicking me against the iron leg of the bed and pounding down on me again. All the air seems to leave the room and everything turns black and I can hear Marie screaming.

'Leave her alone, leave her alone you maniac, you'll kill her.'

He didn't kill me, but something died. Something inside me just shrivelled up and blew away like dust.

Nothing was ever the same after that.

Later I walked across the footbridge and along the unfamiliar, tree-lined roads to the train station with Marie in a kind of silent, slowed-down dream. Sore from the beating and confused by the threats and by what I'd witnessed, unable to make sense of this glimpse of the adult world.

We walked in silence most of the way, both still struggling to hold back our tears, both anxious for the walk to be over. Every shadow and every rustle of wind around every corner seemed to be him, about to pounce. The threats that he wanted me out by the time he got back were still screaming in my head and I knew Mummy wouldn't be able to do anything this time. I pressed my hand over my mouth, to muffle the sound of my crying as we walked, and tried to blink away the image of the two of them I'd seen. I was still trying to work out what I'd done wrong.

Abandoned

We sat on a bench in front of the post office and waited for it to open so that Marie could collect the money that I had to take back in my sock.

'What's gonna happen?' I asked eventually.

'Nothing,' she snapped. 'Try not to think about it.'

Her sharpness surprised me and made me cry again. Marie never shouted at us.

'Please don't let me get sent away, Marie … I didn't do anything … What's gonna happen?' I cried.

'Just keep out of his way. Stay in the bedroom when he gets home and try not to make any noise.'

'I don't.'

'I know. It's not your fault. It's him, he's an animal.'

'Why?'

'He just is.'

Nobody ever knew the reasons for things in our house. But the why's never stopped. 'That's what school's for, and books,' Mummy would say. 'Ask your teachers all those questions.' But the questions just piled up and up in my head like a tower that would one day come crashing down. Marie left school at fifteen to work, and wasn't good at school work, and we knew not to ask her too many questions.

Neither of us had mentioned what had happened that morning and I was still waiting for her to explain it. I sat on one of my hands like I always did when I was trying not to feel anything, watching her as she read the words on the back of her bus ticket. Sandra always said Marie couldn't read properly and that she used to go to a 'special' school because she was 'backward', but she wasn't, and anyway it wouldn't matter because we all wanted to be like Marie when we grew up – beautiful and quiet and kind.

Abandoned

I could smell my uncle's stale, peppery sweat on her shoulder. Out of the corner of my eye I saw the blood crusted in her right nostril and had to fast-blink through the memory of the chaos that had happened in the room after he saw me looking, the way he sprang across as I tried to pull the blankets over my head, ripping me from the bed, with Marie throwing herself in between us the way Mummy did.

'Do you hate him?' she asked.

I shrugged, frightened of having opinions or being 'ungrateful' in case I got sent away.

'I do,' she said, and I stared up at her. Until then I thought what I'd seen that morning meant that suddenly she didn't. But I was glad that she still did; just the way Mummy still hated him. Hate seemed safer the more people who did it.

'Mummy would get really upset if you told her what happened.'

I felt my head lean against her arm and left it there, hoping she would put her arm tightly around me to stop the shake inside, but instead of pulling me towards her she pulled away from me as if I'd given her an electric shock. 'She'd get really upset, wouldn't she? And I don't like seeing her like that, do you?'

I shook my head. She knew I never wanted to upset Mummy.

As soon as the post office opened and Marie had watched me fold the money down inside my sock I wanted to go. I lied, saying Mummy had forgotten to give Liam the note telling my teacher I was going to be late for school. She rustled the large bag of sweets she'd bought with her part of the money and asked me to wait with her

until her train came. I shook my head as the tears continued to stream down, but she cried at my crying, and put an
arm around me and said, 'Please.'

She pulled the bag open and the scented, sugary smell
of Jelly Babies burst out between us into the cold air. We
stood in silence on the platform, biting the heads off the
Jelly Babies, chewing loudly as we watched people bundled
in winter clothes hurrying through the turnstile into the
station.

Marie told me how she wouldn't have to hate my uncle
for much longer because she'd met a boy at work and they
were getting engaged, and were going to live together. I
couldn't tell anyone about that either, she said; that was
another secret that only she and Mummy knew about for
now. I bit a green Jelly Baby in two and chewed loudly,
licking the scented powder from my lips, keeping my eyes
still, not knowing what I could and couldn't look at any
more.

Whatever I did always seemed to be the wrong thing.
'She's a good-for-nothing little bitch,' my uncle would yell
when he wanted me out, and no matter how hard I tried
nothing I did was ever good enough for him. I stood stiff
and awkward, trying to swallow quietly, not knowing
what to do or say, wishing one of the others were there so
that I could copy them.

'Remember those brochures of boarding schools I
showed you?' she said. 'Will you have another look at
them?'

I peeled the Jelly Baby from the roof of my mouth and
held it in my fist. Without looking at her, I shook my head
firmly, my face screwed up in refusal. I couldn't look at
her; *she was going to let him send me away to live in a school.*

Abandoned

All I wanted to do was go home and be invisible amongst all the others. Home, where I belonged, and where Mummy always promised no one was going to force me to leave.

When Marie mentioned sleeping-schools again that morning at the train station I felt everything shake inside. I didn't think about how she might be trying to save me from whatever she had been having to endure at his hands; I just knew that I didn't want to leave the only family I had.

'You would really like it there,' she said. 'There would be lots of girls your age, and they'd all be friends with you, and you'd have a bedroom of your own. You could still come back in the holidays.' But she said it in a lying voice, and I knew it was a trick. 'He's only going to get worse,' she said.

'I don't want to go …' I felt the tears slipping out again, and held my breath until I could hear the blood crashing through my ears. 'Please, Marie, don't let him make me … I want to stay with Mummy … Please make them let me. I don't want to leave … I didn't mean to look. I just woke up and heard noises.'

I never slept in the 'big girls' bedroom' after that night. Stella wanted me back in with her. Mummy didn't know what the fight had been about, but she knew this time he meant it and I had to be kept out of his way, so Stella got her own way again. Marie left soon after, going to live with her new boyfriend Peter and his parents in Leicestershire. A few months later they came back for a visit and to announce their engagement. They brought an engagement cake with them that Peter, who was training to be a chef, had made himself. It was the first time he'd been to the flats, and Mummy fussed around for days getting everything perfect. Sandra was mostly out and I helped Mummy with the housework and getting the girls ready for school and keeping the boys from each other's throats. On the day of their visit my uncle drank more and more and everything was tense. We were playing out later when we heard the loud bangs and shouts. I looked up and saw my uncle throwing the cake in its white box over the landing. I hid behind the burnt sheds behind the washing lines at the back of the square and watched my uncle storming along the landing towards the stairs. All the others were out and neighbours were opening their doors calling, 'What's going on?'

He came out into the square, swearing at the top of his voice, and started stamping on the cake, which oozed out from the broken box before he kicked it up against the big metal bins. Marie and Peter ran down the stairwell at the other end, with Mummy crying and shouting 'Run!' at the top of her voice.

Chapter 12

My uncle called me a 'sneak' or a 'spy' all the time after the morning I saw him with Marie in the front bedroom. Mummy refused to let him send me away, but I ended up getting sent out to the kitchen to stand in the dark more and more; and they were always fighting about it.

'I want her out of here … she's out,' he'd scream, pushing me towards the front door.

'Over my dead body,' Mummy would shout, and sometimes, when he had drunk too much, it very nearly was. He told the girls not to talk to me, that I wasn't their sister and wasn't staying. He told Jennifer, the youngest, never to ask me a question, that if she wanted to know anything she had to ask Stella or one of the boys.

I couldn't shake the memory of seeing him kissing Marie half-undressed in the middle of the bedroom that morning, or how furious he was when he realised I was in the room too. But I couldn't understand what happened either, or why he said he'd kill me if I told Mummy, or why he screamed at me to 'look away' whenever he saw me looking up.

Whenever I saw him after that, even if he didn't shout it, I quickly looked away and sat with downcast eyes;

trying not to think and trying not to see. But everything I did from then on infuriated him. Especially my eyes.

I was used to him making up the rules as he went along: 'Look at me when I'm talking to you,' 'Don't look at me,' 'Don't look at me with those eyes,' 'Look at the telly,' 'Don't look at the telly,' 'Stare at that wall over there until I tell you to stop.' They were never rules that I could learn, so nothing I did was ever right. But I still tried to do everything right; I couldn't put a foot wrong in case he sent me away. But there was nothing I could do about my eyes, and it was them he hated mostly now.

'Leave her alone, you bully,' Mummy shouted back at him. 'What's wrong with her eyes?' But he wouldn't say. Only he and I knew what was wrong with my eyes – all the things they saw that they shouldn't have.

The arguing never stopped. With Marie gone, Mummy couldn't cope with it all on her own. Sandra was the eldest girl then and the one who was supposed to help Mummy out, but she caused even more trouble, skiving off school and being brought home by the police one night for being drunk. Sandra was very different to Marie. Loud and argumentative and fiery; she resented having to stay in looking after us, treating us all roughly and losing her temper at the slightest thing. She was always answering Mummy back and stealing her cigarettes, or money from her purse to buy them. Sandra was very overweight and not pretty like Marie but she had lots of friends, and was always trying to sneak off as soon as my uncle got back from work, to hang out with them, drinking and smoking in the burnt-out cars up by the cemetery.

He sent us out to find her sometimes when Mummy was at her evening job. 'Tell him to fuck off,' she'd say if we found her, and we'd go back shaking, pretending we didn't see her, dreading his anger.

Not long after Marie went to live with Peter, my eyes got me into trouble again. It was raining and my uncle's building job had been cancelled and he came home early. Sandra was looking after us until Mummy got back from work, and my uncle was in his bedroom sleeping. When he woke up and called her out to go to the shop for him she told us not to make a sound or to leave the room until she got back. Nobody did what Sandra told them and the boys laughed at her, calling her 'fatso' and 'acne-face' as she went out, but we all knew not to wake my uncle when he was sleeping. There'd be hell to pay if we did.

Waiting for my turn at snakes and ladders, I needed to go to the toilet. Forgetting her instruction I got up and went out. As I passed his bedroom I saw the light on and the door ajar, and didn't know whether to go forwards or back. I tiptoed past but couldn't help seeing in out of the corner of my eye. What I saw stopped me in my tracks.

He was sitting on the edge of the bed with his trousers down and his legs open and Sandra kneeling in front of him. Instinctively I knew it was something I shouldn't have seen, and after what happened the time I woke up and saw him in the bedroom with Marie, I was terrified of seeing anything else. I tried to hurry past soundlessly, struggling to breathe. But suddenly there was noise and commotion and him flying at me, calling me a bitch and a sneak and kicking and punching me up against the front door.

* * *

Again I didn't know what I saw. Over and over after that day, the scene I saw through the door exploded behind my eyes, but there was no one to tell or to ask about it. Sandra told me she wasn't doing anything but not to tell Mummy, and my uncle said he'd kill me if I told her anything. Every time I was alone with her and he caught me talking to her he hit out at me, asking me what I was whispering, why I was always sneaking about the place. 'She's not,' Mummy would say, 'she's just quiet by nature.' But after I saw him with Sandra he really couldn't bear the sight of me. He wanted me out even more urgently.

'Look at the sneaky eyes on her,' he'd say to get the others laughing. But only he and I knew what he was really saying. I hated having another secret with him, and for Mummy not to know. For days I couldn't look her in the eye. He said he'd kill me if I told her. A hundred times I almost told her – in the way I helped her indoors, the way I peeled potatoes or stood on a chair to clean out the cupboards to make myself useful when the others were out playing so he wouldn't make me leave, or the way I pushed orange tinned spaghetti around my plate, pulling it into half-words that spelled out the truth I wasn't allowed to utter.

One night, after a loud row that the whole landing seemed to get involved with, Sandra ran away from home and my uncle, sneaking back in one morning after he had left for work to take just a bag of clothes and a box of LPs and some money from Mummy's purse. After that there was no one to look after us or to help Mummy. I was still not seven, but I was the eldest girl now.

Chapter 13

Mummy has gone to her new evening job to get some extra money for Christmas. My uncle still hates looking after us, but has had to accept there is no one else to do it now that Sandra has gone.

'Look after them yourself for a change,' Mummy finally tells him. 'See what I have to put up with day in, day out.'

All evening he's been resentful, half-drunk, working up to another argument when Mummy comes home. Our programmes end and he sends us to bed.

'Not you. Here, rinse this,' he says, shoving his empty beer glass into my hand as I try to go off with the others.

From the kitchen I hear him telling the girls I'll be in in a minute. I hand him the washed beer glass and quickly turn to go in through the heavy green curtain that hangs in front of the back bedroom door, which leads straight from the front room.

'Don't fall asleep,' he says. 'I want you for something later.'

'What?'

'Come back in when the rest of them have fallen asleep.'

No one ever says no to my uncle, especially me, but I don't do what he asks. I lie there with the covers over my head, my heart pounding in my ears, trying to force myself to fall asleep 'by mistake'.

He taps me on the shoulder. 'What did I tell you?' he says, his lips close to my ear. 'Come in.'

The front room is silent, the sound on the TV turned down. The news is on and the grey light from it flickers across the walls. He tells me to comb his hair, from the front.

He was always getting us to comb and to pull any grey hairs we saw from his hair. He would give Stella 2p for pulling ten of them. I always had to do it for free, while he snoozed in front of the TV. His hair was greasy and I hated doing it, trying to lean against the back of the settee behind him without touching the red pimples that covered his heavy shoulders and greasy, muscly back. I wasn't allowed to stop until he told me to.

'Pull it into a ponytail and pull it hard,' he would say.

Mummy would sit there telling us not to do it, saying he was an animal and should be locked up. But we put our fingers to our lips to tell her to be quiet.

This time Mummy isn't there and he makes me comb from the front. When I reach up to do it he puts his hands up between my legs and slides his fingers in under my pants and inside me. It happens so quickly I freeze, everything stopping inside me.

'Go in and take these off,' he whispers, pinging the elastic on my pants, 'and put on one of Jennifer's skirts, with nothing on underneath.'

'What do you mean?'

'You know what I mean, now do it,' he says angrily.

But I don't know what he means. I'm not yet seven years old.

'Take off all your clothes and just wear some of their small clothes, right!'

Abandoned

The breath won't go down into my lungs. I go back into the bedroom dizzy with fear, trying to hold back my tears, not knowing what to do, shaking and trying to see through the dark, groping about to find some of the clothes the girls had thrown onto the floor at the end of their bed. I squeeze into Stella's skirt. It almost fits at the waist but is inches too short. I can't do it. I have never defied him in anything he has told me to do, but I can't do this. I don't know why he wants me to do it, but I know that I can't do it. I know that it's wrong, that it's 'dirty'.

I take off the skirt and put my dressing gown on instead. I button it up, but his words 'with nothing on underneath' get louder in my head. I take my arms out of the sleeves and pull my vest off over my head. I take my pants off but I feel cold and wrong and I can't go out there like that. I put my pants back on again and button the dressing gown right up to the top.

'I thought I told you,' he says when I go back out, almost raising his voice.

'None of them fit,' I lie, crossing my fingers in one of the pockets of the dressing gown. 'I nearly broke the zip. Mummy just sewed it on.'

Mentioning Mummy is meant to panic him, but it panics me instead. What if she comes in and sees?

As I circle him, combing his hair from all angles like he tells me to, I see the silenced newsreader on the nine o'clock news staring out at us and I blush, convinced that he is looking directly into the room at us, and that *this* is the news; that he is telling everyone else watching about this, that Mummy, in her evening job somewhere, can hear him saying it.

Abandoned

My legs buckle and the walls of the front room seem to collapse in on us. I feel light-headed and dizzy and take shallow breaths in through my mouth, trying not to breathe in the smell of him. I stare at the shire horses on the mantelpiece, at their shiny black eyes. It feels like I'm not there any more, as if I'm looking down on myself standing in front of him there in my banana-yellow dressing gown with the metal comb in my hand, him lying back in his armchair in his string vest, his red pyjama bottoms gaping open and his thing covered in hair lying out on top of it as he wriggles his rough fingers about inside me, and makes me put my hand on the thing between his legs.

After that evening, nothing and nowhere was safe. And the more he did it the more he hated me and wanted me out of his sight, hitting out at me and screaming at me to stop whispering and 'stop sneaking about the place', as if I was something squirming around in his conscience, driving him mad.

Chapter 14

Marie and Peter come back to get married in the local church. Everyone claps from the landings as Marie walks down to get into the Rolls Royce in the square, while she smiles up shyly and waves. My uncle gets into the car beside her and I frown away memories, clutching my posy of flowers tighter.

I'm a bridesmaid in a lilac satin dress with short puffball sleeves, which everyone says is the perfect colour for me, with my dark hair piled up and studded with daisies. When I see Peter in the church turn and slowly lift Marie's veil, which sparkles with sequins, and put his arms around her to kiss her, I look away in embarrassment. I stare down at two white petals, small, silky ovals edged with pink that have fallen onto the long red carpet in the aisle. A lump shifts in my stomach and the powdery, scented taste of Jelly Babies explodes into my mouth.

I try to blink away the thoughts of my uncle kissing her in the bedroom that morning because I think I know what other things he might have been doing with her, because he's been doing them for months now with me.

* * *

For the couple of days Marie had stayed with us before the wedding I'd been sitting or standing silently beside her whenever I could, hoping that she would tell me something, talk about the secrets that went on with my uncle. But she never did. My silence seemed to bother her and she'd walk off quickly or sit there fidgeting, avoiding my 'sneaky' eyes that always seemed to see too much.

I was confused and ashamed to see her kissing Peter up at the altar in front of all those people. I looked around at the pews behind; everyone was smiling up at them, and I felt my face flush and had to look away. Brendan was staring at me, not at them, and winked, and my blush grew even hotter, my scalp prickling under all my piled-up hair studded with daisies.

Kathy couldn't come over for the wedding; she was coming the following week to take Mummy and me off to Spain for a holiday. That was why Brendan had come over instead. I was even shyer in front of him now, wondering if he was going to do those things that my uncle made me do, or whether he knew about them. I felt his eyes on me wherever I went that day as I swished about in my long satin dress, sounding like Kathy in her pleated skirts with their silk linings.

My uncle watched me like a hawk as well while Brendan was there. I knew he thought I was going to tell Brendan secrets, but I wasn't. I just felt safer next to him. To begin with my uncle told me that Mummy would send me away if ever I told anyone. He didn't have to threaten to kill me – he said that often enough during arguments – but sometimes he said it anyway. He didn't say anything to me at the wedding but whenever I looked he seemed to be there, slipping in and out of the crowd, his little grey eyes following me everywhere.

Abandoned

Brendan had seen my uncle shout at me earlier and thump me for going the wrong way at the gates, and I cried, feeling ashamed that Brendan had seen it. Once my uncle had gone, Brendan came to stand next to me and asked softly, 'Are you alright?'

I couldn't look up at him, but I nodded and he stroked the back of my hand. Later he told me I looked 'gorgeous', 'like a princess' in my long swishing dress. My uncle overheard him and I turned away to go back to all the other bridesmaids standing under one of the pink cherry trees, waiting for the photographer to load another roll of film.

I already felt nervous and frightened around men; now I was disgusted and repulsed by them too. But Brendan was different, he always had been. According to him the Holy Spirit knew everything, so when the sexual abuse started I burnt with shame every time we passed the church on the way home from school, my whole body fizzing with anxiety when I saw the huge, black metal crucifix hanging from the trunk of the horse chestnut tree at the front of the churchyard. The others would stop to knock down conkers, or run in and out of the black metal gates, sprinkling each other with the soft, pink blossom piled under the two cherry trees behind it, while I rushed on worried about the Holy Spirit overhearing all the bad thoughts I'd had about the secret things my uncle made me do.

Brendan didn't like the loud music and disco lights and big glasses of beer in the church hall after the wedding, and when my uncle wasn't looking I followed him out into the car park. He told me to go back in but I wouldn't. Standing next to Brendan made me feel safe, the same way that holding one

83

of the dinner ladies' hands at break-time made me feel safe. No one could get me when I was with them.

We sat outside the church hall in the cream-coloured wedding Rolls Royce with red seats. No one in our family had a car or could even drive so it was always a real treat to be in one, and we talked about driving. Brendan said he would teach me to drive one day.

'Will you teach me now?'

'Come here,' he said, putting my hand on the gears, telling me how things worked and the names of things. 'Sit up here, it'll be easier.'

I stiffened as he lifted me onto his lap, and waited. But Brendan was gentle and kind and it felt nice sitting close to him. He didn't do anything to me or make me do anything to him but my heart was beating fast as I waited for it. When he took my hand from the gear stick and held it tight in his and let it fall on his lap I froze for a second before snatching it away.

'Do you like Vince?' he asked, talking about my uncle, and I shrugged, lowering my eyes, uncertain what the right answer was.

'I don't know.'

When I looked up he had his head in his hands and was crying, his shoulders shaking with emotion. I was shocked. He lifted my hand and put it onto his lap again, looking at me as he did it. I thought he was going to make me open his zip, and my eyes welled with tears.

'It's all right,' he said, taking his hand away, ' I'm not going to hit you. What's wrong?'

'I wish *you* were our dad,' I whispered shyly, checking through the curved mirrors in case anyone overheard, half-shocked I'd said it out loud at all.

'Go back into the hall with the others,' he told me. I thought he knew why I had frozen, knew what my uncle made me do, and what I had thought he was going to do to me too. Of course he didn't know, but sometimes I was tormented with thoughts of how he might have known but had left me there anyway, unthinkable thoughts that over the years swam like fish through my blood, in and out of my brain.

'One day I'll come and take you away from here,' he said again as I got down from the car.

I nodded without looking at him and walked across the gravel with my lilac bridesmaid dress lifted, feeling special and looked after, convinced that he would come back to get me and Mummy one day, but ashamed at the same time to think he cried because he knew about the things my uncle made me do.

Later I told the dinner lady at school – the one whose hand I held in the playground at lunchtime – that one day my Uncle Brendan was going to come and take me away in a shiny cream-coloured Rolls Royce.

'Why a cream Rolls Royce?' she asked.

'That's his car,' I lied. 'He's very rich.'

'That's nice.'

'He's a millionaire,' I said, adding wild embellishments. 'He's coming to get me because I'm his favourite and he likes me.'

'What about your mum, will she just let you go?' she said after a while, smashing the fantasy to smithereens.

'She's coming too,' I said. 'They're going to get married and I'm going to be their bridesmaid, in a lilac satin dress, and look like a princess.'

* * *

After the wedding I went to Spain with Kathy and Sandra. Mummy was supposed to come but my uncle wouldn't let her.

I grew closer to Kathy during those two weeks. I remember the softness of her voice as I lay in bed at night pretending to be asleep as she and Sandra talked. And I remember the light feel of her hands as she gently rubbed sun cream into my skin on the beach, and covered my eyes at the bullfight so I didn't see blood. Little did she know what I saw at home some weekends. I remember feeling confused and disloyal as I sat up close to her in the heat, feeling her gentle hands on me but remembering that all the trouble at home was her fault.

My uncle's violence escalated after we got back from Spain, as did the abuse. Mostly it was me having to do it to him, with my hands and my mouth.

'If you tell your mother you'll have to leave her,' he told me. 'This is a test. She knows all about it, but she's waiting to see if you can keep a secret; to see how good you are. If you tell *she'll* be the one sending you away.'

My head wouldn't take it in. For a long time I couldn't look Mummy in the eye. She would never do that; *she would never send me away.* She hated him. The things she had said went in and out of my head. 'I'm only staying with him for you kids.' 'As soon as you're all grown up I'm out of here.' 'Don't worry, one day me and you are leaving this place. Let them all stay here with him, we'll go away, just me and you.'

At night I lay in bed thinking of all these things, rolling from side to side under the heavy grey blankets, trying to reset all the information in my head. He was lying. Mummy would never be tricking me like he said, 'testing' me, to see if I told. But what if he wasn't?

The others would complain, 'What's she snivelling about now?' 'Shut up, Anya, or we're calling Daddy.'

'Daddy,' the ace always up their sleeve.

Chapter 15

Mostly it happened in the evenings, while Mummy was at her job, but also during the day if she was at the shops or had gone to the hairdresser's or the laundrette. He would call me into whatever room he was in and I would have to do whatever he said.

If she had only gone out locally, and might come back at any time, he took me into the kitchen, turned the light off and sat me up on the draining board, him in front of me, standing up so that he could keep watch out of the window down over the square.

There was no gentleness or coaxing, there was no petting or confusion of feeling, there was just force and aggression and anger and speed. I was just a 'whore's child' and he could do what he liked to me, and if they were going to leave me there, this was how he was going to get his own back. He'd always make me open his belt, pull down the zip and take it out. I'd close my eyes and my whole body would recoil from it; my fists wouldn't uncurl and the feel of it in my fingers gave me the same shock each time, the same jumping out of my skin.

Sometimes my fingers wouldn't work. I would wrestle with the cold metal of his belt buckle, having to push my fingers in under the waistband against his hairy stomach as he breathed in to help me undo it.

'I can't do it,' I would say each time, as if that would stop things.

He would simply breathe in more and tell me to hurry up. I would hear the clank of the buckle falling down against the front of his brown trousers, hoping someone would come in to make it stop, half-hoping one of the neighbours would walk past and see us, half-dreading it, already ashamed, as if it was my fault. But nobody ever caught him. The tearing sound as he made me pull his zipper down was like a rip right through my brain. I was still only six or seven years old, too young to even guess at why he was forcing me to do this, why Mummy was test-ing me, why I was so repelled by it all.

His rough, heavy, calloused hand would be pressed firmly over my small soft one, forcing me to hold it. I would close my eyes, hearing other children playing down in the square, the thump of a ball against the wall outside, the slap of a skipping rope, sing-song voices.

'Like this ...' he had to tell me angrily each time, 'go easy with it.'

But my brain wouldn't keep the information and my fingers always forgot how.

'Pretend it's an ice-lolly, use your tongue on it like that,' he would say, imitating how you'd lick an ice cream. 'Watch your teeth, you bitch. Suck it, don't scrape your teeth on it. Open your mouth wider.' But I couldn't; my mouth was too small, my jaw locked, I was heaving. I didn't want to breathe in the smell or taste of it. At the first taste I would instinctively jerk my head away but he would push it back, forcing me to stay.

'Keep going until I tell you to stop.'

I couldn't breathe. My mind tried to shut off until it was over, to float out of my body, up and away through the window, over the trees and into the sky. But I was always doing it wrong, and he jolted me back with some instruction or warning or slap, and I had to keep squeezing and pulling until it got bigger in my hand, like something waking from sleep, something dirty and stinking and repulsive and alive. Despite having brothers and seeing them naked I hadn't known this thing even existed that changed size and shape and was covered in hair.

When it was finished, or we saw or heard Mummy coming back, he would knock me out of the way, and since I was already crying he would punch or hit me so Mummy wouldn't wonder what my tears were about. Flaring up into rages that I was always too stunned to see coming, he would tell me he'd give me 'something to really cry about' if I didn't stop.

Mummy was used to seeing me cry, so she never had to ask what it was for. He'd hit me for anything and nothing, he always had. But she would still defend me and a new fight would erupt. She would never have guessed the real reason for my tears.

Afterwards, if he didn't want me for anything else and I was allowed out, I would run off as fast as I could across the square so that nobody could see me crying. Sliding in under the corrugated iron fence at the back I'd climb up the railway embankment and roll down the spiky grass, over and over and over until I was sore and dizzy and all his bad had spilled out of me. I'd go to the corrugated iron shelter after, pushing away the weeds that grew all over the entrance, and crouching down inside, trying to sit on the dry bits, to avoid the puddles of brown rainwater, I'd wait for my head to empty.

Nobody came to this bit of the embankment; it was too far. I didn't tell anyone about the shelter or that at the back of it were some of the biggest, juiciest blackberries and tiny wild strawberries. It was my hiding place; the one place my uncle couldn't get me. In the summer I stepped over all the tall stinging nettles, holding my sleeves down over my hands like gloves to push them out of the way, hunting for the juiciest fruit, pushing them around my mouth to take away the taste of him.

When I fell into the nettles I wouldn't tell anyone because Mummy had warned us never to go there on our own, always to go with the bigger children. Once, when I went back with my legs and arms covered in big flaming white spots I tried to hide them but everyone knew where I'd been. I tried not to scratch them or to cry but I got into trouble, and Mummy shouted at me to teach me a lesson, as all the others laughed behind their hands.

That was the day she told us to look for the big dock leaves if ever we got stung and to rub our stings with those.

'They're always there growing by the nettles some-where,' she said. 'Wherever there's bad, there's always good nearby, that's nature's way.'

'Is nature God?'

'I don't know. Now that's enough of your questions. Don't be smart with me, ask your teachers those kind of things, I've got enough to do. Now scram, before he gets in.'

Abandoned

He'd go mad if he saw her paying attention to me. He'd tell her to leave me alone. 'Don't put any of that on her,' he'd said the last time I got stung and she got out the calamine lotion. 'You've got better things to do than take care of her. She's not your responsibility.'

Sometimes, after he'd finished with me, he would give me money. Coins taken from wobbly silver and copper piles on the mantelpiece in their bedroom. I didn't want it. I wish I'd never taken it, but sometimes I did. He would tell me beforehand how much I could have after I'd finished doing what he was asking.

'I don't want to,' I'd say each time, but it made no difference; he made me do it anyway.

'Here, you greedy bitch,' he'd say afterwards, 'take it and get out of my sight.' I'd try to get out of the room quickly. But usually he'd say, 'Where do you think you're going? Clean this.'

I'd have to go down to get toilet paper to wipe him and the sheets with; wiping the gunk from my hands and mouth, trying not to breathe in the smell.

I could never tell anyone else where I'd got the money from. I'd use it to buy an ice-lolly or sweets from the sweet shop, or if there was enough a bag of 'broken biscuits' from the corner shop. I'd run back with them hidden in my pocket or under my clothes so that nobody saw them or my tears, and across to the corrugated iron shelter on the embankment to eat them out of sight of anyone else.

Once, I bought a comic with the money. It was raining and I snuck back to read it in the bedroom while my uncle snored in his armchair with his feet up on the pouf and the paper over his belly. I read it sitting on the big pile of clothes and blankets at the bottom of the wardrobe, the door ajar to let in some light. But the boys caught me and when Mummy came in they said it wasn't fair that I'd got a comic and asked her where I'd got the money.

I couldn't think of an excuse quickly enough. I told her I'd stolen the comic from the sweet shop. I just heard myself say it, almost as shocked as Mummy was. She slapped me across the face, put her coat back on and marched me straight down to the shop. It was the first time she had ever hit me.

'Don't you think I've got enough to do without you playing up as well?'

She made me give it back, forcing me to tell the shop-keeper that I'd stolen it and to apologise. I was burning with shame. I could hear Liam and Michael laughing behind me. I'd counted the pennies out into the man's hand less than twenty minutes before and I knew he remembered me, this pale, timid little girl with her over-grown pageboy haircut and swollen, red-rimmed eyes. I saw him frown in confusion and hung my head so I didn't have to look him in the eye, hoping he wouldn't recognise me. If he did remember, he said nothing. Afterwards, Mummy seemed sorry for what she'd done and sent me and Liam down to the allotments to get an armful of rhubarb from the woman down there and she made my favourite crumble for our tea. I sat there eating it with the others, wanting to tell her with every mouthful where I'd really got the money from, and what he was making me do.

But I knew that she would do worse if I told her. She would send me away, just like he always threatened.

Chapter 16

'Close that door,' Mummy says, and I guess this is going to be another secret.

She tells me Brendan has asked if I want to go to Ireland. My chest tightens.

'I don't want to,' I say, my eyes already filled with tears, 'I want to stay with you.'

'Shhh, it's okay, you'll be able to come back. It's only a holiday.'

'How do you know?'

I mean how does she know about it being just a holiday, but she misunderstands and says she got a letter from Brendan that morning, pulling it out of her cardigan pocket.

'Don't let any of the others see you reading it,' she says, handing it to me, 'I don't want all of them moaning.'

It's only me that's going, none of the others. They aren't to know until the last minute, just like when Brendan comes over to visit. My body is bursting with secrets. Back in the front room the girls are lying side by side on the brown rug in front of the electric fire, watching TV. I sit on the corner of the settee hugging one of the cushions, wondering what another country will be like, excited about seeing all the places Mummy talks about.

Then I start to worry, wondering if I'll really be allowed to come back to England, not knowing who to trust. I feel myself being ripped away from my brothers and sisters layer by layer.

'Don't show me up, will you?' Mummy warns when the day of the holiday arrives.

I shake my head.

'I know you won't … you're as good as gold, you are. I wish the rest of them were more like you. Don't tell them about anything that goes on in our house, it's none of their business, is it?'

I shake my head again. 'No!'

'I'm not having my sister and Brendan looking down their noses at me, thinking they're better than us. They're not better than us, are they?'

'You're better than anyone,' I reply, meaning it.

'Nosy parkers,' she says and smiles, making a game of the complicated relationship she has with her much-loved sister, and we both giggle together. 'If they ask you any questions about what goes on here, just say you don't know.'

We both knew that when she told my uncle he'd say I wasn't wanted back, and he did.

'This time I mean it. I'm not letting them make a fool out of me any longer,' he says, ripping open another beer. 'She can go back to where she belongs … sneaky little bitch … She's not wanted here.'

He wouldn't let her take me to the airport either, saying she had more important things to do, that she had her own children to run around for, not me, and that if they were that interested they would come over and get me themselves.

I concentrated on doing up the zip of my anorak, pretending not to hear him, staring down at my new case with our home address written out neatly on the tag.

'That's what you do in case it gets lost and someone has to send it back,' Mummy told the girls, writing it out in red capital letters.

'Is she coming back?' Jennifer asked, frowning, knowing what my uncle had been saying. 'Daddy said …'

'I know what he said. Don't mind him, of course she's coming back. This is her home too.'

I was feeling very grown-up in my white ribbed polo neck and my first pair of jeans, turned up inches at the bottom because Mummy hadn't had time to take them up.

The night before, when he started drinking, Mummy put up a fight again, saying she was taking me to the airport herself and that was that. But in the end she'd had to back down; there was only so much she could do. Sandra had to come back to take me. She'd made friends with the minicab driver on the way there and wanted to drive back with him. At the Aer Lingus check-in desk she handed my case and my ticket over to the woman in the green uniform and hat who said she would get someone to look after me. Being a minor I had to wear a big tag around my neck with my name on. I was nervous at anyone seeing my surname because I knew that in Ireland it had to be a secret, that nobody was allowed to know it.

Abandoned

The flight was delayed and I sat where they told me, feeling too grown-up for the children's activity pack they'd given me. I didn't open mine. I stared at a small child joining the dots in the colouring book from the pack. She was sitting beside an air hostess, who looked a bit like Kathy, and I wondered what her hands felt like on the little girl's bare arm – wanting and not wanting to know.

Kathy was wearing green velvet trousers and a white silk blouse with frills down the front when she met me at the airport, her long red curls falling over her shoulders, dramatic against her ivory skin and big, soft, slow-blinking, navy-blue eyes. She held my hand as we walked through the airport but her anxiety showed as she looked around her to see if there was anyone there who might know her. She always seemed to know someone.

Going through my case in the car, Kathy put aside most of the clothes Mummy had bought me for the trip, as if they weren't good enough. I told her they were mostly new, but still she took me into a children's clothes shop in the busy part of Dublin where she had already picked out bags of stuff. She dressed me like a doll in a green velvet dress which she told me I was going to be wearing to a medieval banquet at Bunratty Castle. It was a big event and Brendan knew someone who played the harp at it.

I was going to a hotel with Brendan for the first part of the holiday, she told me, and I would be with her for the second part. She drove off the main road to a lay-by and we sat watching traffic speed by, waiting for Brendan. Soon another car pulled up behind us and Brendan got out and came to sit in the back seat for a chat. Then he lifted my suitcase out of the boot and I had to swap into his car. Kathy was nervous in case anyone saw us and guessed I was her daughter. She wanted Brendan to hurry up and leave.

'Calm down,' Brendan said, pressing his hand over hers. 'What am I doing but saying hello?'

But it felt like we were all doing something wrong, like criminals swapping cars in a lay-by, and although Brendan made it seem like fun, and made me giggle, I was already embarrassed by it.

Mummy had wanted to be sure I would say 'please' and 'thank you', and these were almost the only things I did say when other people were around. 'Thank you,' I'd say shyly, sipping black tea like Kathy from thin china cups and saucers as they took me to visit different places and people.

I was introduced as a friend of a friend's daughter over from England, or as one of Kathy's sister's children, depending on who we were visiting. I had to remember to give them a different surname if anyone asked. Over the years I was always a different person's daughter or relative as different people asked. I kept smiling shyly, not speaking, wondering what was happening at home, how Mummy was, and if my uncle was going to let me back, but always keeping my thoughts to myself. Every question was a potential trap. My thoughts slid about and I struggled not to lie while trying not to tell the truth either, answering most questions with a shrug or a smile or an 'I don't know'.

One day while I was there I got to meet my grandmother. Kathy had left her purse at home and we had to drive back to get it. She insisted I stay in the car while she ran in, but I begged to be able to come in just to see what she looked like, and to see the house that both Kathy and Mummy had grown up in, which I'd heard so much about over the years.

She told me my grandmother was very old and ill, and that she looked and acted strangely sometimes; that it would upset me too much. But I promised that it wouldn't and she eventually agreed, slipping her leather-gloved hand into mine as we walked in through the gate. We were just going to 'run in and run out again', she said, and again I had to promise not to say anything to give away my English accent, except for hello and goodbye. I promised and we went in.

'Don't say a word,' she said, squeezing my hand, as we walked into the hall.

'Okay.'

The house was tall and grey and covered in red ivy, and inside it smelt of the sea and cats. Her mother was very ill by then, not bedridden, but frail, tiny and childlike. She became very excited by our unexpected arrival. And when she saw me she stared at me for a long time. I stared back at the almost unlined face with its wet-lipped, toothless grin and eyes that Mummy always said were the same green as mine. And though I kept it to myself, I felt some recognition transmitted in her look. I felt it too by the slow way she reached out her hand and ran her cold, bent fingers along my cheek as she stood there barefoot in a grey-blue silk nightdress which reached down almost to her ankles. She had the same tiny hands as Kathy. She tugged at the combs in her silver hair and it unrolled in waves down her back. I smiled almost idiotically at her as Kathy ran off to get her purse. She stepped forwards, smiling, and asked me my name.

I pressed my lips together, keeping my side of the bargain, so she wouldn't hear my English accent.

Grinning back at her, I shuffled from foot to foot, pulling myself up to my full height, trying to be someone she would be proud to have as a granddaughter. Still smiling, she reached over and lifted a handful of my dark hair, bouncing it up and down on her palm while Kathy continued running from room to room, searching for the purse and calling down to us were we 'alright down there'. Finally, finding it, she kissed her mother and told her to kiss me and rushed me back out to her shiny red car.

As we drove off it was raining hard, splashing noisily against the road and streaming down the windows. And when we turned I twisted around and stared at my grandmother still waving goodbye from the window, looking like a mermaid with her long silver hair unrolled in waves down her back and the long, dark-grey rectangle of sea bubbling up behind the house.

Kathy fired nervous questions at me.

'What did she say? What did you say? Did she ask you where you were from?'

My grandmother died the following year, but I'm convinced she died knowing about me. My tenacity that day in insisting I be allowed to go in to see her is one of the things I'm most proud of.

When I got back to England, my uncle's violence got worse. Maybe he was worried that I had said something while I was away about what he had been doing to me, or maybe he just wanted to ensure I was still as petrified of him as I had been before I went.

He never let up, even on my birthday. The night before there was a huge argument. It was about me again. My uncle said I wasn't allowed to have a birthday, that there'd better not be a single present or card in the place when he got home. We lay in bed listening to them battle it out, Mummy sobbing like a girl, telling him again that he was an 'evil bastard', that she was not standing by and watching what he was doing to me, that she was leaving and taking me with her.

Next morning I told her not to be upset, that I didn't care. His job must have been cancelled because he got home early that afternoon and I could hear them screaming before we even reached the front door. He grabbed me when I went into the front room and started hitting me. 'Get her out of here,' he screamed. 'I don't want her kind in here. I'm sick of the sight of her, get her out.'

It all happened so quickly, but as he kicked me towards the bedroom I saw a white iced cake in an opened box on the sideboard with little pink twisted candles and a big '8' in pink icing, and birthday cards strewn across the carpet. I knew Kathy had sent money for a cake. I wasn't supposed to have it, he'd warned the previous night, but Mummy had bought it anyway. Mummy pulled me from his grip and pushed me into the bedroom, blocking the door with her body so he couldn't come in while I slumped in a daze, sore and bruised and trembling all over.

She came back in later when he was sleeping off his dinner. She was dragging a big blue hamper of presents and told me Kathy had sent them over for my birthday, putting a finger to her lips. That's what he was angry about.

'They're yours,' she said, 'but don't tell the others. Share them out with everyone, okay?'

Her face was red and sore-looking, and she had a black eye, the white all bloodshot. I hated that it was me they'd been fighting about again, Kathy making more trouble for us. She lifted my pillow to show me a hardback children's Bible.

'Shhh, don't let him or the others see this one, this one is just for you,' she said, going quiet and biting her lip as she flipped quickly through its pages.

'Are they true stories?' I asked and she shrugged and nodded at the same time. 'Who told them?'

She smiled and said she didn't know. Making Mummy smile was the best feeling in the world, the way her whole face lit up, and knowing it was just for me. 'Don't let him see it though, okay?'

I nodded and put it back under my pillow, used to God being a secret in our house.

Chapter 17

When I was nine we moved out of the flat and into our first house. It had big leaded windows like all the other houses in the street and huge pink rhododendron bushes in the front garden. There were three bedrooms and a cellar, and a lean-to at the back that opened out to an overgrown garden. It was full of weeds as high as my shoulders, and it was our job to pull them out. My uncle tore off the stiff wallpaper in the kitchen, which he said had mice crawling behind it, feasting on the flour-glue the previous owners had used to paste sections of it back down. He put down traps in the corners with tiny bits of cheese, and went out in the dark with a piece of wood, screaming, trying to batter or scare them to death.

I loved all the space in the new house. I thought it would give me more opportunities to get out of his way, but extra space also meant there were more places he could do things to me, away from the others. The abuse just got worse. No matter where I was he always found me.

Their bedroom was above the front room, and if he was up there and wanted something he banged on the floor with a shoe and one of us had to go up. Usually what he wanted when he knocked down was me.

* * *

The day I walked over the footbridge with the others to visit the house for the first time I was carrying my new Petite typewriter in its little turquoise plastic case. Kathy had bought it for me in Ireland for my ninth birthday. 'You can type whatever you like in it,' she'd said, encouraging me to roll my first sheet of paper into it. But I never could, especially not that day.

I swung it as I walked, listening to a drawing pin stuck to the bottom of my shoe tapping across the concrete, trying not to think about the pain between my legs which was making it difficult to walk. I didn't want anyone to see me wince from the hurt of the day before, when he'd tried to force himself inside me for the first time. It had felt like he was splitting me open. The pain rammed through my whole body, even though he tried to do it bit by bit until I 'got used to it'. Agonising pains that filled my body with screams I could never let out.

I always dreaded being in the house alone with him. One Saturday only a few weekends after we had moved I begged to go with Mummy to the market. He was in a bad mood and there was no one else at home, so I knew he would definitely get me once she was gone and I was terrified.

He'd already said he wanted me there to help with the jobs. 'Please, Mum,' I begged. 'Say you need me to carry things, that you can't manage on your own, please.'

She knew I was terrified of him, I always had been, but I couldn't tell her the real reason I was terrified of being alone with him now.

She looked pale and tired and got annoyed. 'He's in a bad enough mood as it is,' she said. 'I can't keep asking.

And anyway I haven't got spare money for your bus fare.' She needed every penny she had.

He was putting up a curtain rail in our bedroom and I waited on the stairs, hearing him throw tools down into his box.

'No, I need someone here to help,' I heard him say. 'I'm not doing it all like a fool myself while everyone else swans off.'

I was never allowed to 'swan off'. Since we had moved I hadn't been allowed to play out like the others. I had to help indoors with the housework all the time now.

'I tried,' Mummy said quietly when she came down. 'I won't be long. I'll be there and back.'

But she could see how upset I was. 'All right, get your coat, don't mind what he says.'

'Am I coming?'

'Be ready to walk off fast. He'll kill us when we get back though.'

We both stood at the front door ready to go through, my hand on the latch.

'She's coming with me and that's that. I can't carry it all myself,' Mummy shouted up, trying to sound angry. 'Come on, Anya.'

We could hear him shouting, thumping across the uncarpeted room.

'Get back here!'

Mummy pushed me out of the front door, shouting back, 'I won't be long. I know exactly what I want.'

I knew exactly what he wanted too. He was going to try to force it inside me again.

* * *

'Please don't, Dad,' I beg, 'it hurts too much. Please don't …'

'Keep still and it'll hurt less.'

He tries to get me into position on his and Mummy's bed, moving me about, trying to get me to sit down onto him. But my whole body has tensed and he can't move me. His big, dry hand spreads over my mouth and nose and I can't breathe through the pain, my fists grabbing the pillow as he lifts me off and crawls over me, his weight dropping down on me, almost crushing me, suffocating me. His bare, dry flesh everywhere, wriggling about, trying to inch himself into me. My insides not stretching, feeling like I will be ripped apart, as my whole body goes into spasm and my nine-year-old mind slams to a stop.

'Please Dad, I'll do anything …'

He tells me angrily to put it in my mouth then. That's the other worse thing. 'Not that though,' I say, testing his mood.

'What do you mean? What then? You have to do one or the other.'

I have no answer. I just don't want to do either.

'You'll have to do it next time,' he says. 'It won't hurt after a while; it's only at the start. After that you'll get used to it.'

Chapter 18

The second time I went over to Ireland I stayed with Brendan and his family in their big white house outside Dublin, surrounded by fields which sloped down to the sea. His wife and daughters were just told that I was the daughter of a friend of a friend from work, visiting from England.

Like the last time, I wasn't allowed to let anyone know my surname because it was the same as Kathy's. She cut the luggage tag with my name on it from my suitcase and I memorised the surname they told me to say was mine as we drove in from the airport.

'Will you remember it?' Kathy asked with a worried look on her face. I nodded, certain that I would, practising it in my head all the way there. 'It's very important you don't tell them what your real surname is, okay?'

I knew she and Mummy would get into a lot of trouble if anyone found out who I was. They made up some kind of story about me. I think they must have said someone in my family had died, because all Brendan's family held their smiles for ages when they talked to me, and kept asking if I wanted more when we sat at meals, or went to the shops to buy sweets.

'You can have anything,' they'd say. 'Don't be shy, have what you want.'

I remembered Mummy and my manners and not to show her up and I said, 'No thank you, I'm not hungry,' even when I was.

I was supposed to be going to stay with Kathy in a hotel somewhere for the last few days but she was busy, so I stayed on at Brendan's house. His daughters had two horses and a little black pony they'd almost grown out of, which they taught me to ride. During those rainy days, one of them told me I was staying with them a few more days because Kathy's mother had died during the week and she was too busy to take me.

I wanted to tell her that that was my grandmother, but I knew I wasn't allowed to say anything because then she would know that Kathy was my mother. I laughed nervously and wished I could ask Brendan about it, but he'd gone away to meet some clients the day before. I knew I should have been sad about my grandmother dying but we never knew each other. All day I kept seeing the watery image of her like a mermaid standing at the window waving goodbye, with her silvery hair rippling down her back, and the rain streaming down outside.

As we brushed the horses, and Brendan's middle daughter, Caitlin, showed me how to stand with my back to the pony and lift his leg to use the hoof pick gently on him, I panicked. If Kathy's mother was dead, maybe now she would want to keep me there with her? Maybe that was why I was in Ireland. Maybe they had planned it all, tricked me.

As soon as Brendan came back I got him on his own and told him I wanted to go home. He was worried I might have said something about my grandmother and I felt proud to say I hadn't.

'Good girl,' he said, and told me that Mummy was there in Ireland too.

'Can we go and see her?'

'They're both busy with all the relatives and looking after their father. They're both of them very upset.'

But a few days later he told me that we were meeting Mummy that afternoon in Bray. It felt funny seeing her there in Ireland with none of the others around. She looked different, like a stranger, and I felt shivery looking at her in the distance. Her face was all shiny and her short, permed hair was blowing flat in the wind. She was holding it down with one hand and holding the fur collar of her jacket over with the other. They didn't look like her clothes. She was wearing black leather gloves like Kathy's and the same black patent shoes, and her tights were getting splashed with mud as she and Kathy walked over to us.

I wanted to get her on her own to ask her not to go back to London, to stay there, just her and me, just like she always promised me as a little girl.

We walked along the seafront and they gave me money, telling me to go into the amusement arcade as they stood and smoked and talked in whispers. I felt foolish on my own, wandering about the cold dark room from machine to machine with my red cup of tokens, not knowing what to do. I sensed them watching me, saw the strain on Mummy's face and the set look she had when she was lying. I wanted to go and ask her what happened when I left, to find out how bad my uncle's mood was, and if he was going to let me come back again.

Brendan waved and I smiled and walked between the bright machines, listening to all the loud noises and pushing tokens in the slots, trying to spend them quickly. It was no fun on my own. My brothers and sisters would have known what to do, all skidding about the place breathlessly, shouting and laughing. I was lost without them – didn't know what to do on my own, didn't know how to be Anya without them. I always felt like I was disappointing everyone. I could do everything in my head, but didn't know what to say or think or do out loud. I didn't know what I was supposed to feel either, or what I was allowed to feel.

A big, cold feeling swept up inside me. I missed my brothers and sisters and wanted to be amongst them all again, squished up on the settee, eating pick 'n' mix and laughing at cartoons, one of them again.

The wind had died down and we sat at a table outside a café under a big green umbrella. I had a cheeseburger with onions and Coke with ice, and the others had big sugary triangles of apple pie and cups of tea. Mummy asked me if I'd enjoyed my holiday. I wanted to lie and tell her that I hadn't, that I only liked being with her, because I knew that would make her smile. But the other two were watching me and I felt shy, so I nodded. When she asked me what I'd done I told her about the horses and Brendan's children, and how Caitlin was teaching me to ride.

'Are we flying back together?' I asked, excited to be going on a plane with Mummy. She lit a cigarette and told me she couldn't come over with me, that she had to stay a few days more, and I'd have to go back on my own.

The cheeseburger stuck in my throat. I washed it down with some Coke and tried to keep my face blank so the other two didn't know what I was thinking. The light disappeared from Mummy's face. I could tell she knew what I was thinking, that I couldn't go back there to my uncle on his own. But of course even she didn't know the real reason I didn't want to be on my own with him.

'It'll only be for a few days,' she said, crushing her cigarette out in the ashtray Brendan pushed over to her, 'then I'll be back.'

I had pineapple fritters after my burger and ate them slowly, trying to hide my fear and not to 'let her down' or 'show her up'.

'Can't I stay here until you go back?' I asked later, following her to the toilets, but she said they were all going to be too busy with the funeral arrangements.

I still had some tokens left and when I went back I tried to get the pennies to fall off the cascading machines, my eyes welling with tears as I stared hard through the scratched glass, seeing all the coins hanging off the edge, about to fall with the slightest nudge. I could see the reflection of the grown-ups huddled together behind me, playing shove-a-penny with my nerves. *I can't go back there on my own.* When I finished my tokens and went back to them, Mummy said Brendan had a surprise for me.

'How would you like to come over to Italy with me for a couple of weeks?' he asked. 'I can get the time off and I could do with a holiday. There's a lady who lives there I'd like you to meet. She's a niece of mine, you'd like her. She's always got her nose in a book like you too. I'm just a show-off really, I want to show you I know someone with brains.'

'Italy?' I said, looking at Mummy, trying to read what she was thinking from her face, and trying to remember how far Italy was. Then I remembered the long boot shape of it on the map on the classroom wall.

We were meant to be in Italy for two weeks, just while Mummy helped Kathy with things after the funeral. But at breakfast near the end of the second week Brendan asked his niece Caroline, who we were staying with, if she would look after me there for the rest of the summer. I couldn't breathe. I knew it was all a trick; that they weren't going to let me go back to Mummy. I stared up at Brendan helplessly, too shy to say anything in front of Caroline.

Brendan somehow persuaded her, without consulting anyone in England when he went back to Ireland. I stayed there for the entire summer. Mummy didn't have a phone so I couldn't speak to her. Nobody seemed to think about how being away from my brothers and sisters and Mummy for all those weeks, not knowing if I could go back, would affect me.

It was a hot summer and Caroline had to drag me around with her everywhere she went, constantly grumbling, 'I wish this summer would roll on.' She wasn't used to children, especially frightened, mistrustful ones, and kept saying she wanted me to go home, in a way that hurt behind my ribs.

When Brendan eventually came back we met him at the airport, standing at the glass watching him coming down the steps of the plane like a movie star, his jacket looped with one finger over his shoulder and his tie loosened in the heat, which rippled silver across the runway. It reminded me of watching him coming across our landing at the flats on hot days in summer. And how much I wanted to go back home.

Although it was hot Caroline said I could wear the new, green, Italian coat she'd bought me, with the pleat down the back, to show off in front of him. She'd taken me to my first proper hairdressers too. When he saw me his eyes widened and he asked me for a spin. I did as he asked, knowing the back was swinging from side to side, the way it did in the mirror, and I tried not to let them know how pretty I felt, and how much like all the other girls.

'You look like a different child altogether,' he exclaimed. 'Are you sure you are the same one?'

On the last day I had my portrait drawn in my new coat by a small oriental man on the Spanish Steps in Rome. Brendan was taken aback when he saw it, unrolling it onto the café table, weighting the ends down with the salt and pepper pots and his hands.

'Do I look like that?' I asked.

'He's made you look far too old,' Brendan said. 'It's the way you'll look when you're about eighteen … it's the look your mother had.'

I didn't know which mother he was talking about.

Chapter 19

When I came back from Italy the arguments and violence grew worse. He made it clear that he didn't want me back and didn't like the changes in me. Maybe he was fearful again that I'd told someone about what he'd been doing. Maybe he also resented the fact that I'd been allowed a break from all the abuse, and that I could almost look him in the eye again. My brothers and sisters seemed to have grown used to me not being there for a whole summer too. He told them not to talk to me, that I wouldn't be staying long, that I wasn't one of them and didn't belong there.

I knew my brothers and sisters were just jealous of my 'holiday' and so I didn't talk about it, trying to put it out of my mind and settle in amongst them again. But my uncle's ridiculing began again. 'This is not a hotel,' he would say at any opportunity. 'You're not in the Ritz now.' And my brothers and sisters would snicker behind their hands with him if he wasn't too drunk yet, as Mummy told them all to leave me alone.

The sexual abuse didn't take long to start up again either. From visiting Brendan's house and Italian families with Caroline, I now knew how other people lived, knew that this wasn't 'normal'. No one in their houses banged down on the floor for little girls to go up to them.

The only thing that changed was that he seemed to think he had to hit me even harder, to be certain I would never tell Brendan, or anyone else, the truth. I was used to being hit, to having 'busted lips' and nosebleeds, and bruises over my arms and legs from his punches. The bruises were usually disguised by my clothes so there wasn't much anybody could see, like the pains between my ribs when I breathed or lumps the size of eggs on the side of my head from when he threw or kicked me out of his way. But it was harder now, getting used to it all over again.

When he called or knocked down on his bedroom floor with the shoe for me to go up I would shake inside and sit there trying to ignore it, praying that one of the others would give in before me and go up instead, hoping he just wanted a fizzy drink for his hangover or a pen to do the Pools with or some soap for his bath. We would squabble between us until he banged down again. Usually I would have to go. Sometimes one of the boys would jump up saying, 'It's you he's calling, not us,' but I would pretend not to hear and sit rigid on my hands, crossing my fingers under my thighs until they came back down. They always came down saying the same thing: 'Daddy said you have to go,' or 'Daddy says he wants the black comb. You have to take it up to the bathroom to him.'

I'd find the comb and put my arm around the bathroom door, waving it through the steam, saying, 'Catch, I'll throw it in.' Trying not to see him, or breathe in the stench of him.

'Hand it in to me,' he'd say.

'No.'

'Get in here.'

I'd go in looking anywhere but at him and he would laugh at my nervousness.

'Stand there.'

Sometimes I had to just stand there and he'd make me watch him while he soaped himself. 'Keep your eyes open,' he'd say. Other times he'd make me wash him myself. I had to soap him all over as he lay back. Usually he'd close his eyes, so I would try to do it without looking, pushing the sponge across his skin, trying to avoid going between his legs, but he'd never let me avoid it. If he'd been washing himself, he'd lie back afterwards and tell me to comb his pubic hair. I'd shake my head but he would make me.

'Look at it,' he'd laugh, lifting his pelvis out of the scummy water and forcing me to open my eyes. Through the curls of darkened hair I would see his penis lying there, soft and discoloured and repulsive.

'Touch it.'

I would pull the comb through the short hair, trying not to touch him, trying not to look, staring at the black mould speckled on the wall above the door where the strips of stiff, flowery wallpaper were coming away from each other. Or, if he made me look at it, I'd look at the dark mole high up on the inside of his right thigh. I was always crying when I did it.

'You can't say it's dirty after you've washed it yourself,' he'd say.

'It still is,' I would remind him, as I did whenever he asked me if I liked it.

'No,' I'd say.

'Why not?'

'It's dirty.'

'You'll like it one day,' he would laugh.

* * *

I usually had to wash his hair too, squeezing the washing-up liquid he used for it into my hands and scrubbing his scalp hard as he knelt up in the middle of the bath with his eyes closed.

'Watch what you're doing, you bitch,' he'd say, wiping his eyes as suds slid down. 'What are you trying to do, blind me?'

When he was ready to get out I would hold the towel out and then dry him. I would try to dry the other parts, the stretches of rough, pimply skin, trying not to touch between his legs. But I never got away with it. He would wrap the towel around his waist, shake his wet hair like a dog, and go up to the bedroom carrying a bundle of his clothes, telling me to clean out the bath and come up.

I would stay in the bathroom or tiptoe downstairs hoping he'd forget it, but he never did. He'd call me from the top landing, and I'd say I had to get some cleaner for the bath, or I'd just taken the wet towels down to the laundry basket.

Spreading the towel on the floor he would make me shake talcum powder between his legs, handing me the red, square tin of Imperial Leather from the mantelpiece. I had to smooth it over his penis too, then he would lie back on the bed and make me put it in my mouth, telling me how clean it was now and not to complain as I heaved at the taste and gagged for breath.

My mind wanted to float off, but a bit of me always had to stay there listening out for Mummy coming back or for one of the boys spying outside, or one of the girls coming up and catching us. I always had to be ready to jump off the bed.

* * *

The more he did it the angrier he seemed to get with me afterwards. Maybe he was battling his demons and losing. Maybe he didn't know how to stop, so wanted me out of the way to give him no choice. My shock and tears just seemed to amuse him.

After a few of Kathy and Brendan's visits came and went, he saw that he could do anything he liked to me again and that I wouldn't tell. He clearly enjoyed humiliating me too. Once, his brother, Shaun, had come back from a holiday abroad and given him a pack of playing cards with pictures of nude women on the back, and a pen with a woman who became nude when you turned it upside down.

'I'm not having things like that in my house, there are children here,' Mummy shouted. 'I want those out.'

His brother just laughed at her and my uncle kept them. When the others had gone upstairs he made me stay there and play. Mummy was only upstairs in the bath. He shuffled them and made me play snap with the picture backs, forcing me to look at them. I burnt with shame as I put down my cards on top of his. If he won I had to kiss him, with his dirty, beer-stinking breath.

'Open your mouth,' he said, putting his rough tongue – like thick sandpaper – into it, the shock of it stopping me in my tracks.

'What's wrong with you?' he asked, smirking. 'Don't you like it?'

'No,' I cried, trying to pull away.

'You will,' he said as he shuffled for another game, laughing at my tears.

* * *

Abandoned

Sometimes he did actually throw me out of the house, pushing me through the front door at the height of one of their rows. Mummy usually stopped him, or unlocked the door again and forced me to run up to the bedroom while she took the brunt of his fury.

One night I got a real taste of how much easier and calmer life would be for Mummy without me there. During an argument I'd been called back out of bed and asked again who my father was. Brendan had been over just a few days before, and I'd gone to the hotel he was staying at that looked out over Tower Bridge to have lunch with him as a birthday treat. None of my brothers or sisters had treats like that, so it wasn't fair, and I usually paid for them afterwards.

Again that night I said I didn't know who my father was when he asked, trying to get me to tell him it was Brendan. As usual, he didn't believe me and tried punching a different answer out of me. Mummy had told me a long time ago that it wasn't Brendan and her word was enough. I never had to ask again.

She tried to make him leave me alone, but he had other reasons for hating me then, for wanting me out. Maybe he didn't know how to stop what he was doing to me, and with me spending days with Brendan in a hotel, who knew what secrets I could have told? His paranoia was driving him mad. In the end he pushed me outside in my nightie onto the street in the pitch dark, screaming that he never wanted to set eyes on me again, reminding me that I didn't belong and that I wasn't wanted there. Maybe that was the only way of stopping himself now, to have me gone.

I ran up the wet road, barefoot, up on tiptoe, almost blinded by tears. I felt fear and shame at the thought of the neighbours seeing me. I didn't know where to go, which direction to take. I heard the door shake in its frame and the scrape of the top bolt being pushed across, and behind it Mummy's screams faded away.

Hearing the argument die down in the house as I walked away made me think that that was what it would always be like if I wasn't there. Mummy's life would be peaceful. I stumbled up the road towards the smear of the streetlights near the boarded-up church at the top, my tears unstoppable, not able to bear the pain in my head or the thought that I was the one who caused all the trouble for Mummy just by being there.

I didn't even dare to stop when I eventually heard Mummy calling out my name and, turning, saw her running up the road in the dark after me. She'd got her tweed winter coat on over her purple velvet dressing gown, and was carrying a coat for me. She put the coat and an arm around my shoulders, trying to push my feet into some slippers of Stella's, pink ones edged with a roll of dark-pink fur, and sizes too small for me. I gripped them onto my feet with my toes and we walked on, crying into each other.

Mummy stopped to lean against a wall, crying loudly and dragging on a cigarette she'd found in her coat pocket. She looked pitiful, broken, all the fight knocked out of her, making my tears fall even harder. All I could do was listen helplessly, absorbing the pain: *Please, Mum, be strong, don't give up now, not now.* I rubbed her shoulder awkwardly through the rough tweed of her coat, feeling each of her sobs deep down in my bones, not knowing what to say. Then she crushed her cigarette against the wall and cursed him through her tears, saying she was going back, vowing she wouldn't let an animal like that lock her out of her own home.

'You go,' I said, 'I can't ...' But she took no notice and made me go back with her.

We walked back and she picked small stones out of the wet soil under the bushes and threw them up at the windows to get one of the others to come and open the front door. She tried to calm me down as she prised my fingers from the gate. I'd wet myself, hot pee sliding down my legs and soaking Stella's pink slippers as we eventually walked into the hall, both shaking.

Next time Brendan came over I took the day off school and Mummy and I met him in the restaurant at the back of BHS. They discussed the secondary schools I might go to. Brendan wasn't familiar with the English school system and asked Mummy about grammar schools.

'Has she a chance of getting in?' Brendan asked.

We weren't really the type of family that got into grammar schools. Mummy lit another cigarette, and picking loose tobacco from her tongue said, 'That one's got brains in places you and me don't even have places,' which made Brendan laugh and me blush.

Mummy was always saying that proudly about all of us, whenever we tried to show her how to do long division or fractions or spell big words. No matter how hard my uncle tried to knock me senseless over the years he never could. What neither Mummy nor Brendan had realised, though, was that I would have to pass a test in verbal reasoning.

'What's that?' Mummy asked.

'Speaking out loud.'

Abandoned

I wasn't good at that. I was too shy and it took too long to filter out all the things I wasn't allowed to say, all the secrets. I always let my brothers and sisters do all the talking when anyone was there, and kept quiet in class, just like Mummy always told me to. 'You're there to learn, not to make friends,' she'd remind me if she found out I'd been bullied again.

I had mixed feelings about going on to the 'big girls' school.

'Pull up your top, let me look at you,' my uncle says, cornering me in the kitchen the night Brendan goes back.

'No.'

This time he is in a good mood and laughs at me. 'Pull it up. I want to check to see how big you're getting.' I turn away but he reaches across and pulls my top up himself, then lifts my vest, rubbing his big, rough hands over my still-flat chest as I cringe away from him. He makes me pull down my pants to show him if I have any pubic hairs growing yet. I can hear the TV in the other room, and someone upstairs in the bathroom walking about, and out of the window watch the cat walking along the high fence between the gardens.

'It won't be long now,' he says, tugging at my nipples again. 'I can put them in my mouth and suck them then. Would you like that?' I wipe at my tears and shake my head, still refusing to look up at him. 'Kathy likes that. She's always wanting me to play with hers when she's here,' he says. 'Did you know that?' I freeze, as he laughs. 'She loves it,' he says. 'She can't get enough.' *Everything he says is lies …*

* * *

Abandoned

In the end I got a '1' in English, a '1' in maths but only a '2' in verbal reasoning. For the grammar school you had to get a '1' in all three. Instead I went to the big girls' secondary school in a blazer two sizes too big and a green kilt skirt down almost to my ankles. A girl called Heather who lived in one of the new maisonettes at the back of the shops went there too. Both of us were book-mad and we waited for each other by the lamppost at the top of her road with our noses always in our books.

We were in different classes, though, and when she went off at the bell I felt lost. Sometimes I wouldn't talk to anyone until I met her on the walk home again, but I didn't care; I didn't need friends outside.

'There are enough of you here,' Mummy always said. 'You all have each other.' That was all I needed, that and Mummy and books.

Chapter 20

The boys *know*.

Recently he has been very lax. I've heard their footsteps outside his bedroom, heard the loose floorboard outside it creak, have felt them there, daring each other up the stairs to stand outside the door to listen. I can't bear that they know. It is another layer of abuse on top of it all.

A few times they've even burst in, and I've jumped off the bed while my uncle shouts, 'Get out! What are you doing in here?' But he never sees them until it's too late.

'Sorry,' they say from the landing, making excuses about something they were looking for.

For a few months they've been hinting at things.

'What do you do when he calls you into their bedroom?'

'What do you do when you go into the bathroom with him?'

'What do you use the black comb for?' they say, laughing at each other.

The ground shakes under me.

'Nothing, I just give it to him.'

'Yeah, right! It doesn't take half an hour to give him a comb.'

'What else are you doing in there?' Michael says, to make Liam laugh.

'Nothing … cleaning the bathroom, tidying up the mess after one of you've been in there probably,' I say, trying to get them off the subject.

'Yes you do, we know.'

'Know *what*?'

They tap the side of their noses, knowingly. 'We're telling Mummy.'

My chest hurts. I can't breathe. I fight back tears. 'I don't do anything.'

'Why are you crying then? Whore!'

'*What?*

'You heard.'

They make the rude, squelching noises at the sides of their mouths that they have been tormenting me with for weeks now, to imitate the sound of masturbation, driving me from the room blushing furiously.

If they tell Mummy she'll make me leave, make me go away, not him.

He's been getting too casual about it. He even makes me touch him in front of them sometimes. He did it last night, when Mummy wasn't there. We were all in the front room; the boys were in the armchairs and he was sitting on the sofa behind them with my sisters and me. He told the girls to sit on the floor, and after a while motioned for me to sit closer to him. I shook my head. I knew he couldn't say it out loud in front of them, but when he did it again I had to obey.

He had his red pyjama bottoms on and a newspaper over his lap. He grabbed my hand and pulled it under the newspaper, in through the slit in the front of his pyjamas until it was over his soft penis. My hand recoiled but he pressed his big rough hand over mine and forced me to hold it. I sat there paralysed with fear and revulsion, pretending to watch TV, hardly breathing.

'Pull it,' he whispered.

I defied him, doing nothing. He couldn't shout it out in front of the others.

'Pull it,' he repeated, under his breath.

I tried to move my hand away.

The girls tried to find excuses to look around. 'What did you say?' Stella kept asking, looking over her shoulder.

'Nothing,' he said. 'Watch the TV.'

But she kept looking around. She wanted me to sit on the floor with them but he wouldn't let me. 'What's she doing?'

I yanked my hand away and shook my head at her.

'Turn back around,' he told her angrily, 'or go up to your bed.'

I clenched my fist and tried to resist his pulling my hand, but he yanked it back over and made me continue masturbating him under the newspaper. I could hear the noises terrifyingly loud: the sound of my hand pulling; the loud rustling sound of the paper on top as my knuckles knocked against it; the sound of my heart and the blood pounding in my ears. It was all so loud. I felt certain the others must have known what was happening. I kept my eyes on the backs of their blonde heads – the girls like twins with their waist-length, white-blonde hair down loose over their shoulders, and the boys a darker, sandy-blond colour like him. I watched all of them at once, tuned into them, ready to pull my hand away if any of them made the slightest move to look around. Every now and again the boys passed looks between each other – serious, knowing looks – but no one turned around again.

He's done it before like this in front of them. But last night was different; he tried to make a game of it, tried to make me like it. He sent the boys down to the off-licence to get more beer.

'And get Coke and crisps for you all.'

There was excitement all round at his generosity. He told the girls to go too. Stella said it was too cold and she didn't want to, but he said she had to. I had to stay there. 'There's a job I want her to do.'

Once they were gone he made me put my legs up at the side of the mantelpiece. I tucked my school skirt in between my thighs, trying to hold it there, over my knees, but he pulled it down and stroked the insides of my thighs.

'Do you like that?'

I shook my head.

But for the first time in my whole life with him, he was almost gentle, stroking instead of pulling and pushing aggressively.

'Is it ticklish yet?'

'No.'

But something different had happened. I was getting some sensation in my legs, some ticklish feeling when he ran his fingers along my thighs. It shocked and frightened me. I felt betrayed by my own body. I didn't want any feeling at all with him, and I sensed that he was crossing another line, trying to get me to enjoy something that had repulsed me ever since I was that little girl he sat up on the kitchen sink at the flat, fumbling with his zip as he kept lookout.

When the doorbell rang he let me swing my legs back down and get myself neat and back into position. He went to open the door, saying, 'Follow me up to the bedroom when I get up to go in a few minutes, okay?'

I couldn't look at the boys when they came in, but I felt them looking at me. I sat there blushing, staring at the adverts on TV, pulling open the packet of smoky bacon crisps Stella had handed to me.

I didn't follow him up later. I sat eating the crisps, almost swallowing them whole, feeling the sharp edges scrape the back of my throat on the way down as I struggled to hold back my tears; repulsed by the smell of him on my hands. Trying not to think what the others were thinking. A few minutes later he called down from outside his bedroom and I had to go up, as the boys snickered and made the squelching sounds of masturbation.

As the abuse got worse and he became more casual with it, the boys picked on me more and more, calling me a 'slave', a 'slut' and a 'prostitute' under their breaths. Words they would never dare say if Mummy was there. Words that stunned me.

Chapter 21

Saturday mornings have always been the same in our house, until this one. My uncle has long gone by the time we get up. Mummy works all day, just a few roads away, starting at nine and finishing at five. She gets up first and then calls me and we both get dressed quietly and go downstairs, having our breakfast together while the others sleep.

I love that part of the day, my time on my own with her once a week, just me and Mummy together pottering around making tea and toast, putting the radio on low for the news, drawing the curtains back to let the sun fill the rooms, the back door opened for fresh air. A safe, normal start to the day – before my uncle comes back and gets me on my own.

The girls go swimming with one of their friends from school. The boys sometimes get the bus down there later, or play football at the top of the road with their friends, after they've helped me with the jobs, ready for inspection when my uncle gets in at midday. The house has to be cleaned from top to bottom on Saturdays. My uncle goes mad if everything isn't done by the time he gets in. In the afternoon it will just be me and him. That is how it usually goes.

Abandoned

On this Saturday at the beginning of May, when I am still a few months away from my twelfth birthday, the boys are refusing to help with the housework, taunting me about the things they claim they have seen me do with my uncle. 'Rude' things that probably both disturbed and confused them, but also amused them. Things they accuse me of liking, of wanting to do.

Over the years he has encouraged them to tease and ridicule me, to treat me the way he treats me, and this is just another thing to tease me about.

'We know what you do. We've seen you, we know!'

'Know *what?*' I ask again, ashamed. My whole world tumbling down.

'With Daddy … We're telling.'

My heart stops each time. *Mummy can't know.*

Liam is less than a year older than me, and Michael almost two and a half years older than me. Both of them are at secondary school, but too young themselves to really understand what they have been seeing, or what they have been tormenting me about now for months. They know it's something wrong, something unspeakable, but this is our house; this is what happens in it. Nothing is said outright, just loaded questions and innuendoes, hints and snickering, half-accusations and, when it suits them, whispered threats that they will tell Mummy if I don't get the housework done, as they run out early to play football.

But the strain of having someone else know, of having all this half out in the open, is unbearable.

Usually I don't say anything, I can't. But this morning, a few months after they first began their teasing about it, I scream at them to be quiet. I never normally scream; I'm the quiet one, all the spontaneity and boldness knocked out of me over the years. But their teasing about this on top of everything else is too much, and I crack.

Instead of helping me clean the house they create more mayhem, throwing food and cushions at each other and tearing around the rooms aggressively, fighting or threatening each other one minute then turning on me to try to impress each other, making one another laugh by tormenting me, telling me they will tell Mummy what I do with him. Just boys being boys, their father's sons. But this time I really think they will tell.

Running from room to room after them I demand to know what they mean, what they're planning to tell her.

They run out of the house, elbowing past me in the hallway, mocking my tears. They say they're going out to play football with their friends at the top of the road and I'd better have all the jobs done by the time my uncle gets back in, or there'll be murder. 'Slave,' they call from the front door, 'just do it.'

'We're telling anyway,' Liam calls back.

When they've gone I collapse, sobbing, in front of the gas fire in the kitchen, and am not prepared for the waves and waves of emotion that come. I don't know how to stop it. He'll be in soon and nothing is done. I can't manage on my own, and don't know if they are really telling Mummy. I have to get them in to help me straighten the house in time, and to find a way to stop them tormenting me, a way to convince them that I don't want to do those things to my uncle, that he forces me.

I am shivering, crying uncontrollably, but I have to confront them; it's the only way to get them to stop.

I open the front door and, squinting into the bright sun, call them in. They are humiliated at a younger sister calling them in in front of their friends and refuse, but eventually they come, full of bravado, shouting back at me that I am going to get it if this isn't good.

Once they're in the house I plead with them to stop saying that stuff. I tell them that he makes me do those things; that I don't want to. They don't want to hear it but it half comes out … someone now knows about all that vile, repulsive stuff. All the secrets that I have been carrying around for years. I have put something into words … broken through the years of silence. And when I do, I can't put it back in again. I just implode, rocking backwards and forwards in floods of tears, my head in my hands, struggling to breathe. *I didn't mean to tell them. I just wanted them to stop.*

Liam stops bouncing the football. They both look at each other and the room goes icy cold. It must have dawned on them that they have stepped over a mark. We all have.

'Shhhh,' one of them says, but the tears and shaking won't stop. Everything blurs, goes in and out of focus, dark and light … dark and light. The ornaments on the mantelpiece look like they are about to fall, sliding about, and the ground won't stay still. The boys shout at me to stop crying. But they don't tell me how to.

I hear them say 'please', and promise they will never say anything about it again. I can hear the fear in their voices, and it makes me worse. Michael shouts that my uncle will be back from work any minute and that he'll guess what's wrong. 'We're all gonna get it if you don't stop.'

But it is all out of control. I am shaking, my head is wobbling and I can hardly breathe. It feels like a million ball bearings have been set off inside me from my head to my toes and I am trembling all over. Inside, I scream at myself to keep still and to stop crying but the tears won't stop, coming in streams of mucus from my nose, my eyes almost sealed with them.

My uncle is going to kill me …

Their reminders that he will be back any minute only make it worse. The emotion of all those years floods through me. All those years of violence and threats, all that terror, that fear, those drunken nights of being dragged out of bed, forced to sit on the settee and listen to talk of my 'whore of a mother'.

All those years of absorbing Mummy's pain, trying to be invisible and not a 'troublemaker', as the others some-times called me. All those years of having to hold it all in, and now here it all is crashing out of me, and I don't know how to stop it or what is happening to me.

Michael slaps me to stop me from crying hysterically, but I still can't. I can hear what they're saying about it killing Mummy, about her maybe leaving us if she finds out, about social services taking me away.

'The whole family will be split up if they find out,' Liam says.

I can sense their panic and want to stop, but none of the ways to control my thoughts or my body work any more. All I know is that my uncle is going to come in any minute, and that I have to get out before he does. If he sees me like this he'll know I've been talking to the boys about it, or he'll guess from their behaviour. I have to get out, he'll kill me …

'I have to go,' I stutter. 'I'm telling Mummy I want to leave.'

'You can't.'

'I have to.'

'What are you going to say if she asks why?'

'I don't know …'

They plead with me not to go, the way I pleaded with them earlier about their teasing. They try to frighten me more by telling me how much it will upset her, how she'll probably leave us or have a breakdown, how I will be taken away.

I can't breathe. His key will be turning in the lock any minute and I have to get out of here before it does.

I make for the door but Liam holds me down while Michael guards the doorway, his arms stretched across, looking stunned and skinny and frightened at my new-found physical strength.

But in the end, when I promise that I won't tell her why, just that I want to go over to live with Kathy in Ireland, they let me go. She knows that the boys have been picking on me more than usual recently, encouraged by my uncle, copying him, using any excuse for a fight.

Michael stands aside to let me pass, but I can't stop shaking and my legs won't cooperate. I beg one of them to come down to her office to tell her for me.

Michael walks off, refusing. 'I'm not being part of this,' Liam says when I plead with him. But in the end, after I promise again that I won't tell her the real reason, that I will just tell her I want to leave because of their teasing and picking on me, he comes.

It has been the constant threat hanging over my whole childhood – that I will be sent away from Mummy – and now here I am asking for it.

Chapter 22

Mummy is on the phone, smiling. There's a Biro behind her ear, and only one other person in the office, a grey-haired woman in a pale-pink jumper, with her back to us.

The office where she works on Saturdays is in a tiny, mock-Tudor building tucked away at the end of a small parade of shops a few roads down from ours. It has a big, plate-glass window, and we stand outside waiting for her to look out. Liam tells me through clenched teeth to stop crying, that it'll make Mummy worse. They know I'd jump off the edge of the world for Mummy. But now that the tears have started I can't stop them. Not even for her.

We aren't meant to disturb her at work on Saturdays, except in an emergency, and we rarely do, but if we have to, usually she'll beckon us in. Looking out at us today, she obviously senses something more than the usual fights and bickering has happened. When she's put down the phone she comes out, her lighter in one hand and an unlit cigarette in the other. By the time she closes the door she is already crying. Seeing her standing there, so helplessly, sets off more panic in me. She's always telling me I'm 'too sensitive', and not to let things bother me so much, but she must realise this is something different.

'What have you done to her?' she yells at Liam. Then, looking back at me shuddering, unable to look at her, tears streaming down her face as I sob, she is trying to force me to tell her. But I can't. I'm not allowed … *he'll kill me*. Eventually I manage to get out through shuddering, stuttering sobs that I want to go.

'Go where?'

Hyperventilating, shoulders heaving, gasping for breath, the words hiccupping out through gulps of air, I finally get out that I want to live in Ireland.

She's stunned. She can't believe it. Of course she can't. Not after all those years of having to whisper me secret assurances that no one would ever take or send me away from her.

'Why?'

'I just want to.'

She tries to get me to tell her why, but I can't get any words out or look up at her. Her crying is unbearable. She doesn't believe it's just because of the boys' teasing. I'm eleven and a half now, and when my uncle isn't there I can stand up to the boys. She knows it has to be something else. I feel like I'm going to collapse onto the pavement.

'What's happened, what's caused this now? I want to know the truth, Liam,' she says angrily. 'What have you done to her?'

'Nothing,' I say. 'I just … I just want to go. Please, Mum … I don't want to stay at home any more. Please phone Kathy …'

Her crying is as loud as mine. 'What have you done to her?' she says, shaking Liam by the shoulders. 'What have you done?'

'Nothing,' Liam says.

'Tell me, Anya, what have they done to you? Just tell me.'

My eyelids are flickering shut and my head feels like it is cracking open with pain. *Any minute he'll be here.* 'Tell her, Liam,' I say in the end. I don't know what else to do to get her to let me go.

Liam shakes his head.

'Tell me what? I'm warning you, Liam, tell me, what is it?'

I can't say it, can't put it into words. 'Tell her, Liam … so she'll let me go.'

Nobody breathes.

'Daddy has been doing things to her.'

'Things? What things?'

And in the silence that follows the penny drops and she knows.

The colour goes from her face. She stares blankly at us.

Then she breaks down, crying, saying, 'No! When? Where is he now?'

'Just let me go, Mum, I'm alright,' I say, looking over my shoulder. 'I won't tell Kathy … I just want to go.'

But Mummy won't agree. She knows I don't want to go.

'Please, Mum … he'll … please … he'll kill me.'

Nobody knows what to do. Liam stands rooted to the spot, still a head taller than me but looking thin and small, standing too still, his hands curled into fists at his side. Mummy pulls out another cigarette, her face white and puffy, her eyes wild and staring. My right knee spasms; nothing inside me will stay still. Everyone and everything is falling apart.

'What's gonna happen, Mum?' I ask.

But she doesn't know. We all look at the pavement, trying to shush each other, none of us touching or know-ing what to do. Eventually she pulls herself together and promises that when Marie and Peter arrive they will know what to do. I still can't stop crying or shaking, even when someone Mummy knows walks past. I wish someone would hold me.

Since having their baby, Marie and Peter have been visiting us about once a month. They come up on the train and pop in to see Mummy at work first as it's closer to the station. They won't get to the house for a few hours yet.

'What'll happen then?'

She doesn't know any more than we do. She says until they come we have to go back up to the house and pretend nothing has happened. But we can't go back up to the house, not now, not after this.

'Please don't make me, Mum … please … I can't. He'll kill me when he knows.'

She's sobbing like a little girl. 'Don't let on, just pretend everything is normal. Do it for me, Anya, please.' I would have jumped off the edge of the world for Mummy. *Poor, poor Mummy* – the shame of it all, of having all our private business told on the street, of having to tell Marie and Peter, of having her sister know that she has let her down, that she hasn't been able to look after her daughter for her the way she promised her she would all those years ago. She doesn't know what to do. She reaches out to push my hair from my face but I jerk my head away – I can't let myself respond to gentleness. I have to close myself down, not open myself up.

'You have to go back there,' she says, 'go back and act normal until we come … Don't let him guess anything … Do it for me.' She is crying into her hanky, her hands trembling. 'Say you and her had a fight, Liam,' she tells him. Her voice hardens. 'Do you understand?' Liam nods, without raising his head. Standing there, her words 'Don't give anything away ... Just pretend everything is normal ...' echo in my head.

It's what I would try to do for most of my life after that – try not to give anything away, just pretend everything is normal.

Chapter 23

from the moment my uncle comes in he knows there is something wrong. He's late, but not in a bad mood, and I hear him talking to Liam in the hall, joking. When Liam stays quiet I hear him asking him what the matter is; have we had a punch-up? He doesn't wait for the answer; he is used to that. He hangs his jacket over the banister and kicks off his heavy, steel-toed boots. I try to keep out of his way, but they will come into the front room any minute, so I have to slip out past them. He's still holding on to the door frame, pulling off his boots. He's blocking my way. I shake my hair across my face and look down at the carpet, not wanting him to see the swelling and blotches or the look of terror on my face. But he reaches out and grabs my arm.

'Are you the go-go dancer?' he says, pulling me by the wrist, trying to make Liam laugh, which usually he would. I freeze. I can smell the drink from his breath. I bite the inside of my cheek hard but my tears are starting again.

'No,' I mumble, trying to pull away. 'Marie and Peter will be up in a minute.'

He kicks his other boot off. 'Is that this week?'

Liam nods, and my uncle lets go of my wrist. 'What's wrong with you?' he asks, but I'm past him, going down into the kitchen.

Abandoned

'Bring in my slippers,' he calls. 'Was this hallway hoovered?' I call back quickly that it was and can hear him laughing with Liam and saying something about me as they walk into the front room to watch the start of *Grandstand*.

'What's up with her?'

'You know what she's like.' Liam's voice sounds cracked and tiny. The fear in it makes me shake. I get my uncle's brown tartan slippers from under the chair in his bedroom and bring them down. He knows our fight must have been a bad one, but he's used to fights between us; he's been encouraging Liam and the rest to pick them with me over the years. But this time he seems worried, a bit nervous. He doesn't keep to routine; he doesn't even inspect the housework; and his keys and newspaper are still on the bottom step out in the hall.

When I walk in I overhear him asking Liam again what has happened, but my tears are coming so I put his slippers down at his feet and half-run out of the room. He's trying to make Liam laugh.

'Did you give her a few right hooks? What did she get – a busted lip?'

When the jobs are all finished I try to keep out of his way, but the house suddenly seems tiny. A clap of bright white light seems to go off in my head; I feel dizzy, and don't know where to go. He can get to me wherever I try to hide in this house, he always does, especially on Saturday afternoons; Saturday afternoons are guaranteed. I push open the door to the cellar and sit in the musty gas-smell at the top of the steps in the dark with my knees to my chest, under the coats hanging from hooks on the back of the door, my fist in my mouth to muffle the cries.

Abandoned

Not being able to hear what's going on is worse. My head is pulsing. Any minute he could burst in. I go back and mop the kitchen floor, sloshing the red tiles with water, but the sun streaming in through the windows dries them too quickly. The minute I hear footsteps coming I mop it again so it's soaking and shiny, like a moat of red blood that nobody can get to me across. Even my uncle doesn't step over wet floors; he'd come back and get me later when it was dry. I slosh and slosh until the muscles under my arms tire and I can't hold the mop any more.

When Liam comes out to get my uncle another beer from the fridge he won't even look at me. He's shut me out already. His face looks like a corpse, his eyes empty and staring, with dark smudges I haven't noticed before on the skin underneath. The way he looks scares me. He steps past quickly as if I'm not there.

'What's happening?' I whisper. 'Does he suspect anything?'

'You've gone and done it now,' he says, without looking at me, throwing the tea towel back onto the draining board.

I feel sure that he is just about to go in and tell. 'Please don't say anything, Liam,' I call after him quietly, 'please … I never wanted any of this to happen. I just wanted you and Michael to stop calling me names.'

He doesn't answer.

I tiptoe after him, straining to hear over the wrestling on the TV.

'Was it a bad one?' my uncle laughs. 'Did you win?'

When he starts snapping open another beer I run upstairs.

* * *

Abandoned

On my pink bed under the window in the corner of the bedroom I share with the girls, I can't stop trembling. I try to rock myself still, stuffing the edge of the pink counterpane into my mouth to muffle the sounds of crying. I know any minute he is going to realise what has happened. Through the sounds of the rain gunning down outside and *Grandstand* coming up through the floorboards, I wait to hear his footsteps thumping up the stairs two at a time.

All afternoon, jumping out of my skin at every noise, I wait; trying to keep an eye on the road to see if anyone is coming, my face pressed to the glass to peer further down. I feel drowsy and my head feels too heavy, like I am slipping in and out of consciousness. I don't hear the gate open or the footsteps up to the front door. When the doorbell goes my heart leaps into my mouth.

I think I recognise Marie's voice. I can't hear Peter, but then Peter is always quiet. He doesn't like my uncle; he sits there reading a newspaper until my uncle goes up to have his sleep in the afternoon. Jack must be asleep in his pram. Through the floorboards I hear the horseracing on the TV, and Marie saying stuff now and again. Why is she just chatting? Why isn't she coming up to tell me what's happening? I knew it; this is all a trick – a test, just like he always said when I was a little girl. He'll be up to get me any minute.

It's already gone five. Mummy will be here any minute. My teeth are chattering and I can't stop shivering. Someone eventually comes to the toilet on the half-landing below. *It's him.* I reach up for the window latch and think of jumping out. Then the bedroom door pushes open. It's

Marie, with her finger to her lips and her shoes in her hand. I break down when I see her. She tiptoes across the carpet and puts her hand over my mouth, telling me to shush. She's crying too.

'Don't cry. I can't let him see my make-up run,' she says. She wipes her mascara with the hem of her blouse. 'Just keep normal, please Anya, just for a bit longer. We can't let him know anything is up. Mummy's at the police station and the police are going to come. They're going to arrest him,' she whispers.

No air will go down into my lungs. The reality terrifies me. 'When?'

'I don't know, but I need you to do me a favour. Mummy said if she wasn't back by quarter past, to go to the chip shop and get chips for tea. He'll start to get suspicious in a minute when Mummy's late, start wondering why. We just have to act normal so he doesn't think anything's up. If he doesn't get his tea in time he'll just drink more.'

She presses a folded piece of paper with the scribbled order and a five-pound note into my hand.

'Make one of the boys go, Marie, please.'

'No, you have to.'

'Why?'

'Mummy said … Please, Anya. It's okay, look, come on, go behind me. I'll cover you.'

I half-crouch behind her as she goes down the stairs, stopping at each landing to listen out. She grabs my blue anorak from the coat rack and gives it to me behind her back then moves across, blocking the doorway to the living room to let me run past the other side of her.

My fingers won't work properly and I fumble with the lock, sure that he's at my back.

Abandoned

'Quick,' Marie whispers, 'run.'

I don't stop running until I reach the chip shop roads away. It's empty and I slam the door behind me, out of breath, everything inside me shaking, convinced he's run after me.

I'm in a daze as I walk back with the food. Then I see the two police cars part-way down our street, blue lights flashing against the pavement and the big, pink rhododendron bushes, but I'm almost on top of them before I've seen them. I stop dead. They're parked just outside our house. I see a group of people crowded at the gate, and the dark-blue uniforms and hats of the policemen. I'm just seeing pictures; my mind isn't back in my body yet. Then I realise what's happening. I turn to run, but hot pee dribbles down my thighs. I cross my legs, squeezing my muscles inside, trying to make myself stop, and dive into the neighbour's garden to hide, crouching down behind the privet hedge, the chip bag crushed to my chest.

'Is this her?' I hear someone say.

There are footsteps to the gate; I'm trapped. If I run out now I'll run right into them. 'You've gone and done it now,' I hear Liam's voice say inside my head. The gate swings open noisily and four navy-blue legs bend down.

'Hello, are you Anya?'

Curled up tight into a ball I won't say a thing. They lean down and take my arm away from around my head, trying to coax me up. I drop all my weight downwards, digging my heels in and leaning back, trying to lie down. *He's going to kill me.* They force me up but I cling to the gate, the fish and chips falling open to the ground. They pull my other arm. I'm afraid I'll snap. One of them picks up the bag of chips, kicking the fallen ones away, and they lead me by the shoulder back down to the house.

Abandoned

The front door is wide open and he's there, standing in the narrow hallway against the green flowered wallpaper. His big, heavy hands are curled into fists at his side. They want me to walk past him. *I can't. I won't.* There's another policeman, taller than him, standing next to him, but my uncle is still belting out orders, telling Michael to get his 'proper fucking shoes ... Not them ones, you halfwit,' throwing back the ones Michael has already thrown down to him, the brown suede slip-ons with tassels on the front. The policemen are standing there waiting, but my uncle isn't afraid of anyone.

When he throws back the shoes he turns and sees me. I shrink back towards the door and flinch, but one of the policemen stands in front of me.

'Move over, let her pass.'

I fly upstairs, shaking from head to toe. Marie runs up after me.

'It's all right; they're taking him away now. It's all right; he's going ... Animal!' She screams the last word down from the top of the stairs. 'Hope they lock you up for good.'

I put the chips on the bed. 'Sorry ... I dropped them.'

'That doesn't matter, forget them.'

I can't stop shaking. Marie makes me change my socks and underwear.

'Why?'

'They want you to go to the station too.'

'I'm not going.'

'You'll have to. You just have to tell them what he did to you. Then they'll put him away. Mummy is there waiting.'

We can't find clean underwear. The laundry isn't done until Sunday, when Mummy and I and one of the others take it all down to the launderette. I find clean socks and pull off the damp ones.

I beg Marie to come with me but she can't. She says she has to look after the girls. I don't know if they are back from their friend's house yet. I didn't see them, or Liam. She says she has to make arrangements.

'He'll kill me,' I say. 'He'll get me.'

'He won't. I promise. You'll go in different cars.'

She tries to lead me downstairs but my legs won't move. The police promise that I won't see him.

'The car taking him has already gone,' they say. 'Look, you can see it at the end of the road.' I see the end of it disappearing around the corner past the newsagents. 'And we'll drive a completely different way there.'

I'm sandwiched between two policemen on the back seat. One offers me sherbet lemons from a paper bag but I won't take them. They try to talk to me, asking ordinary, everyday questions, but I don't know what to answer, afraid it's all just a trick. I can't bear the thought of them all knowing what he's been doing. It's a secret. It had never been put into words until the boys started teasing me about it. They promise me it will be all right, that I won't bump into my uncle on the way there.

'Slow down,' I plead to the driver, 'please go slow.'

When we get there they lead me in from the car, but when we come around the corner there's another car pulled up just before us. And he's there, his hands behind his back, his head lowered, being led in handcuffs.

I won't move. That clap of bright white light goes off again inside my head, and the hysteria that has been

Abandoned

locked up in me all day starts to erupt. I cling to the black drainpipe on the corner, refusing to take another step. My uncle raises his head and for a moment holds my stare. It sinks deep down into my brain. I'll get you for this one day, his eyes are saying.

Chapter 24

It was only a few seconds, but I feel as though he has been looking at me like that forever.

The police lead him away through the small side door into the station. I can't move. They're prising my fingers from the drainpipe one by one, but softening their voices, saying, 'It'll all be alright.'

'Your mum's inside waiting for you,' they say. 'Come on now, Anya, let go, it's okay.' I can hear impatience in the taller one's voice. 'This is silly,' he says, squatting down beside me. 'Come on now, we don't want to force you. But you've got to come in with us.'

They promise that I won't see him again; that he won't do anything else to me. They say it was a mistake, that I shouldn't have seen him, that the car he was in must have got delayed somewhere. They promise me that Mummy's waiting for me inside and that they're bringing me to her, not him. I don't trust anything any more. They've tricked me; this is all a trick. I know they're lying again.

Somehow they get me to go in. We stand at the end of a long, blood-red corridor, quiet and dark after the lights in the car park outside. There are doors along both sides, doors which could fly open any time and him leap out. It's too quiet. I won't go forwards.

'Show me where she is,' I say. 'Please, just let me see her first.'

One of them goes off reluctantly, his hat under his arm, his boots echoing loudly down the empty corridor. It feels like I must have fallen asleep for a moment standing there, because one of them taps me on the shoulder and says, 'Look, there she is.'

I drag my head up from my chest, my eyes flickering open, and see Mummy in one of the doorways right at the end. She's like an apparition with the light fanned out behind her, frail and tiny, standing there with her beige mac still belted.

I stumble towards her, crying loudly, convinced that he is going to jump out from one of the other doors and get me. Poor Mummy. Her face is bone-white, her eyes bloodshot and swollen from crying, her hands shaking, wringing white tissues. I throw myself at her, burying my head in her chest, saying, 'Sorry, Mum, I'm sorry,' as she puts her arms around me.

The interview room is empty apart from two white tables and some orange plastic chairs with cigarette burns. A window, with painted white bars on the outside, overlooks big steel bins under sheds opposite. Mummy's grey leather handbag is on one of the tables, and cups and saucers and a half-empty bottle of milk are on the other one, next to some blank sheets of white paper. Another policeman sits down and shuffles them straight.

All I can think is that my uncle is somewhere in this building, and that I have told. After all his threats and warnings over the years, *I told* ... That, and the way Mummy looks.

'We're just going to ask you a few things about what he did to you and you can answer them.'

I don't want to. I can't. All these years I have never put anything into words. Now I've said too much already.

'It'll be all right, Mum will be in the room. You just have to tell us what he did, then we can make sure he never does it again.'

How are they going to make sure? This is my uncle they're talking about, my uncle who can do whatever he likes. I look up at Mummy to see if it's okay but she's turned to light a cigarette. I shake my head.

'It's okay, isn't it, Mum?' they say, and Mummy nods. She's crying loudly into a tissue, refusing to sit down, pacing around, up and down the room, saying she feels sick.

'I don't want to, Mum. Do I have to?'

There's a long silence. 'It's all right. Tell them,' she says.

I can hear from the way she says it that it isn't all right. Nothing is right now. I turn back around in my seat and listen to her draw on her cigarette, her crying getting louder as a policewoman locks the door.

They're easy questions to start with, about what time I got up that morning and what I had for breakfast, what time Mummy left, where everyone else was, how many brothers and sisters I have, their names … Then they start asking questions about him.

I don't know how long it goes on for. The ashtray is full and Mummy is still walking up and down, chain-smoking, her face twisting in pain. I am not going to say any more; I can't make Mummy hear any more of this. But they keep on.

Abandoned

'Take your time,' they say. 'It won't be much longer. Just a few more questions then you and mum can go home.'

They carry on, asking when it happened and where everyone else was at the time. They want to know how many times, how many years. What did it feel and sound and smell like? What did it taste like?

I don't know – nothing ... dirty ... disgusting ... bad ... it made me heave ... *I don't have words for these things.*

They push for descriptions, saying they know how tough this is, and they promise it will be over soon, but just try to tell them, describe it properly. Was there anything semen tasted like? How much of it was there? How thick was it? What did it feel like? Was it like anything else?

How do I know? I'm not even twelve ...

I've got one ear on them and one tracking Mummy behind me, walking up and down at the back of the room, sobbing loudly. When I answer more questions Mummy doubles over, retching into the tissue. Nothing comes out, but she goes for the door, trying to unlock it, saying she can't listen to any more of this.

'Your mum's going to stand in the corridor,' they say, 'just outside to get some air. Is that okay?'

But I'm frightened of letting her out of my sight. I don't know what she's thinking – or where my uncle is.

This is all my fault.

'Sorry, Mum ... Please stay with me, Mum, *please*, I'm sorry.'

But she lunges for the handle, rattling it loudly, saying, 'No, I can't stay, I can't breathe ... let me out. I have to get out of here.'

* * *

Abandoned

When she comes back in, a policewoman rubbing her back and plucking tissues for her from a box, they start again.

'What else did he make you do?'

I swallow back the taste of sick from the back of my throat and look up at Mummy. I can't get any words out. But they coax them out of me: about the things he made me push inside him while he masturbated – the handle of the yellow screwdriver or parsnips or the red plunger which I sat beside that afternoon inside the cellar door. I tell them about having to push it in until I was frightened he would rip open; about hitting him with his belt, his trousers around his ankles as he bent over the bed telling me to do it harder; or kneeling on the bed on his hands and knees, showing me how to push them in as he masturbated over opened-out page threes spread all over their double bed, or made me masturbate him.

They ask me about the pictures, but I always tried not to look at them or what he was making me do. I would stare outside into the trees as my hands moved, or his moved inside me, until he would turn around and thump me, saying, 'Watch what you're doing; keep your mind on what you're doing.'

They ask me why I thought he asked me to hit him with the belt, but I don't know. I tell them that I was frightened of hurting him, that I didn't understand why he would want me to hurt him, why anybody would.

The bald one is shaking his head, as tears fall onto the backs of my hands in my lap. I can't lift my head to look at him. I am too ashamed.

* * *

Abandoned

Mummy leaves again and I hear her crying outside, moaning loudly like she did after some of the worst arguments. It sounds even worse here, echoing in the long corridor, with strangers sitting opposite me hearing her, and me the one causing it this time. They say they have to wait until she comes back again. 'No wonder you were frightened of coming in and bumping into him,' one of them says. 'Don't worry, this will all be finished soon.'

They sit there awkwardly, glancing up at each other and around the room, asking if I want a drink. I take a sip of the cold water and blow my nose with the tissue they hand me. I stare at a big Kit-Kat box sticking out of the top of one of the bins outside; I'm sure I see something move behind it. *My uncle could be anywhere … waiting.*

When they've finished, the bald policeman reads out what they've written down and makes me sign each sheet of paper. It's the first time I've signed my name anywhere, and for years after, whenever I have to give a signature, memories of this day are there in my fingertips.

A lady with red shoes and long blonde hair to her waist like Marie's arrives and we follow her downstairs to a room with a bed. While the blonde woman snaps on rubber gloves, the policewoman tells Mummy that the lady is a doctor and is just going to have a quick look inside me.

'Why?' I ask Mummy. 'I don't want anyone to.'

I lie on the hard bed, feeling the feathery ends of her hair brush against my hands, my knees up. I have been crying so much my eyes are almost sealed closed but I feel everyone looking at me and burn with shame. She smells

Abandoned

of flowers, and the cold she brings in with her clings to her jumper. I feel her long, sharp nails through her gloves. I can't blink the lights straight. She asks me some questions, and when she takes off her gloves I watch her write some stuff down on a clipboard and then shake her head at the policeman who has come in from the corridor and is towering over me.

When she asks me when the last time he was inside me was, I'm silent for a long time because I can't remember, and I don't want to remember. I shrug and she scribbles something down. I never get to tell her it had been at least a couple of months. The last time he did it I bled, and I think it frightened him. Next time I told him that Mummy saw the spots of blood in my knickers and wanted to know where it was from. He makes me do things to him now instead. He says I'll be ready soon.

Chapter 25

Marie met us outside the police station in a taxi. Suitcases packed with some of our things were in the boot, and somebody had lent her money for the train fares. Marie had arranged everything. We were not going back home; we went to King's Cross to get the train up to her house in Leicestershire. Everything in my life had changed in a moment. The girls had gone ahead in another taxi with Peter, and were meeting us there. The boys had stayed behind somewhere in London with one of my uncle's brothers.

Everything seemed to be outside our control. We were all unprepared for the fear and shock of what had happened, overwhelmed by it. Mummy and I were trying not to cry on the train so as not to attract attention or upset the girls, who weren't being told what was going on, just that my uncle had been taken away for hitting me.

We had table seats to ourselves at the end of a carriage, but there were other people nearby and Mummy and Marie whispered over the girls' heads. Mummy's tears set mine off again and neither of us could stop. It was late and the girls were tired, but they had a new packet of felt-tip pens and colouring books, and I watched their blonde hair slide across the table as they filled in the same picture of a clown standing on a beach ball, juggling sticks. Marie put her finger to her lips and whispered to me not to cry because I was upsetting Mummy.

When Peter came back from the buffet car with bottles of Pepsi, and crisps and Mars bars and tea for Mummy and Marie, we were still crying. I glanced over at Mummy, trying to make her look up at me, but she wouldn't. I felt cold inside and alone; ashamed that she now knew all that stuff. 'Why don't you go outside in the corridor with Peter for a bit, to get some fresh air?' Marie said, putting her arm around Mummy.

I didn't want to, but I went. Peter and I stood there for ages without talking, bumping together now and then and pulling away awkwardly as the train rattled on, both of us staring through each other's reflection in the black windows as we tried to make out the dark shapes of the countryside speeding past. I knew Peter didn't know what to say. But I didn't either.

I wished somebody would hold me. 'Do you want one of these?' he asked, taking another two Mars bars from the inside pocket of his leather bomber jacket. I nodded that I did, but when he passed it to me I threw up into his hands. He wiped his jumper at the small silver hand basin in the toilet, and I turned around sleepily to watch Mummy and the others through the sliding glass doors. It felt like a dream, seeing them there like that, watching their lips move without being able to hear them, seeing them all huddled together, Mummy's white cigarette smoke streaming into Marie's loose blonde hair, Jennifer in denim dungarees asleep across her lap, the little ladybird on the end of her gold hair clip sliding down past her ears, her felt tips rolling without lids across the sticky, map-blue table.

Abandoned

None of us had ever been to Marie's house before – except for Mummy, on the day Jack was born. And although it was late we took our shoes off and lined them up at the back door the way she showed us. With our anoraks still on, we followed her in a daze from room to room as she showed us around. She pulled pillows and bedding from the airing cupboard at the top of the stairs, and made up the spare bed and a put-up bed in the back bedroom overlooking the long narrow garden. I could see through the dark that it had a badminton net across it and shuttlecocks lay on the black grass. Nothing else seemed to be there, and I tried to cover my jumpiness, but every movement and every unfamiliar sound felt like my uncle lying in wait for me.

The house was tiny and spotless, like a doll's house, with everything neat and in its place. There were white panelled doors with brass handles and soft pink carpeting in every room and up the stairs. I had the put-up bed while Stella and Jennifer slept head to foot in the spare bed next to Jack's cot, with its Winnie the Pooh covers to match the wallpaper. But I couldn't sleep. *What if my uncle had escaped?*

I went downstairs to tell someone I was feeling sick again. I just wanted to be with them, suddenly frightened of being on my own. But I didn't know how to make a fuss, or tell someone what I was feeling. I confused the hallway with the one in our house and bumped into the coats hanging on a stand by the front door, thinking it was someone standing there waiting to get me – my uncle about to pounce. I shivered and tried to blink away that look from earlier – the way he lifted his head slowly from his chest, and looked up at me sideways in the car park as he was led away in handcuffs. That look that was there when I closed my eyes for years afterwards.

Marie gave me a towel and the red washing-up bowl to put at the side of my bed in case I threw up during the night, and I went back up, hurrying past the coats without looking. I wished I was like the girls, the age when some-one could pick you up and hug you. Grown-ups were always awkward around me; I was never the type of child people took to, my uncle's treatment of me made sure of that. I was too withdrawn, too wary and distant, my eyes too full of secrets. Marie came up again later with a hot water bottle and said if I needed anything else to call down but I never did, not even when I woke up during the night and, forgetting about the bowl, threw up onto the new pink carpet by mistake.

The next evening our Uncle Brendan came over, which seemed to make Mummy even more upset.

'What am I going to tell him?'

As I pressed Lego bricks into place on the breakfast bar with Jack, I heard Marie telling her she had nothing to be ashamed of, that none of this was her fault. I felt myself blush and look away, wondering if they thought it was all mine. There was lots of talking in the kitchen when he arrived. The others drank coffee with him while we were sent into the front room with a big glass bowl of crisps to share, to watch TV and play with Jack. Later, Brendan came in to say hello. He always shook my hand when he first arrived, but this time he just sat next to me and said, 'Are you okay?'

I nodded.

'I heard what happened,' he said after a minute and I nodded again, staring at the TV, blushing bright red. I hated having anyone know.

I didn't know what Mummy had told him – how much? How much she'd told anyone.

For nights and nights they were up talking, trying to make plans about what to do next. During the day there was lots of staring at me, until I looked up and then everyone looked away. Everyone was kind and treated me nicely, but nobody talked about it. I was left alone with my thoughts, having to force them all back down, push everything back in, like the girls did with the red jack-in-the-box in our bedroom at home.

Sometimes as I passed someone in the hall or took things into the kitchen they would ask if I was all right and smile, and I would smile back shyly, nodding, unused to being the focus of attention. I could see that everyone was uneasy around me. The feel of the room would change when I walked into it. But nobody was fighting or shouting and everybody was being nice to me, and when I woke at night pouring with sweat after bad dreams I was allowed to go and sit downstairs, and sometimes Marie poured me a cup of tea to bring back up.

But nobody talked about what happened. They never have, ever. Years later, when I asked Brendan why no one talked to me about it from that day on, he shrugged and said they thought that if they didn't talk about it then I would forget it. They didn't want to remind me of it, he said … they thought that was best. We were a family used to not talking about things, used to sweeping problems under the carpet.

We stayed at Marie's for a couple of months in the end. None of us belonged this time, not just me, and for a change not belonging brought us together rather than set me apart. Everyone treated it as a bit of a holiday at the beginning – there was no school and none of the old routine to keep to – but it all felt a bit fragile, ready to shatter any minute. Every time a door banged or there was a sudden loud noise, I'd swing around expecting the peace to be ripped apart. There were no chores to do at Marie's. Suddenly I was a child again, with just books and games and playing with our nephew Jack, who laughed at everything; and no men except for Peter and Brendan, neither of whom shouted or bullied. And none of the things my uncle made me do. All of that was over. Though it was years before I trusted that.

We went on outings, me and my two little blonde sisters in our new cork-heeled sandals. Sometimes we all dressed the same, like triplets, in new clothes Brendan bought us from C&A – petrol-blue boiler suits with zips up the front and racing-driving patches sewn onto them: Ferrari and Silverstone and Marlboro. We walked into the town centre with Marie on Fridays to do the weekly shop in our new outfits, thinking we were the bee's knees. My two little sisters and I inseparable, as it should be, Stella no longer the boss now that my uncle wasn't around.

Brendan bought bunk beds for us, to put in Jack's room. 'They can easily be dismantled again,' I heard him tell Peter. But he never mentioned when that might happen. Nobody did. All of us were adjusting to life without my uncle, growing new skins, nobody mentioning him, not even the girls. Not having to do the housework as I did at home, I was almost a child again: playing badminton on the long summer evenings and chasing my sisters around the long narrow garden; reading *The Little Prince* to the girls on the kitchen step until it was too dark to make out the words; brushing their long silky hair as we watched TV on the black-and-white portable in Marie and Peter's bedroom. Meanwhile, Mummy was falling apart downstairs; I tiptoed around her, not understanding why she had changed towards me, why I seemed to be upsetting her so much – thinking it was all my fault.

Kathy came over for a few days and all I remember is her sitting in with Mummy whispering and crying most of the time. When she and Brendan went back to Ireland, Mummy got worse. She wore sunglasses if she came into town with us. Her head shook and she was jumpy and weepy and kept the girls around her like bodyguards whenever I tried to sit or be near her. I knew instinctively it was her way of trying to put all that vile stuff she'd been forced to hear at the police station out of her head, and I knew to keep out of her way, but it still hurt to feel her pulling away from me.

During the day, indoors, she sat in the front room with the curtains drawn watching TV, living on Silk Cut and milky tea and her nerves. When she passed me to go to the bathroom one morning after getting a postcard from the boys asking when she was coming home, I smelt drink on her breath. I smiled at her but she looked away and went off, wiping tears. She looked terrible: cold and bony. Everything was my fault.

I didn't know what to do with myself. I kept waiting for something to happen. Everything made me jump. I laughed it off, but every shadow and every sudden movement was him, lying in wait for me. But after the first time, when I ran in breathless, slamming the back door, sure I'd seen him crouching behind the wall at the bottom of the garden, I didn't tell anyone.

'He's not there,' Marie had said. 'They're not letting him out. And anyway, don't worry, he doesn't even know where I live.'

After helping Marie wash the soup bowls from lunch I asked her if I could bring Mummy in her cup of tea. I put a small plate of Rich Tea biscuits on the arm of the settee, but she didn't even look at them. I stood there staring at the TV. It was *Crown Court* again: all the serious-looking men in grey wigs and black gowns in the wooden courtroom. I plumped up the cushions and wanted to ask Mummy what was going to happen now but I didn't want to remind her of it all. Instead I just asked if she wanted me to open the curtains. She shook her head and took a sip of her tea, and then took headache tablets from the white tub on the shelf behind her and knocked them back. I didn't know what else to say, standing there feeling foolish and lonely and shut out. I wished I could make her smile the way the girls could. 'Is there anything else you want me to do?' I asked, standing awkwardly in the doorway, but she had already closed her eyes and slid down on the settee with one of Jack's blue baby blankets pulled up over her.

'Is Mummy okay?' I asked Marie when I went back out.

'She'll be alright. She just needs a bit more of a rest.' I watched her wipe tomato soup from the top of the cooker and fill the kettle again. 'No … actually I'm getting a bit worried about her, to tell you the truth. I might give the doctor a call,' she said, lowering her voice so the girls didn't overhear.

Deep inside me something shook. 'Why?' I asked, spinning around.

'She's started drinking during the day and can't stop crying. She can't go on like that much longer. She'll have to go back to London soon. Everyone has to get back to school.'

I asked if there was anything I could do to help.

'Just keep out of her way, and let her see you're okay. That's the best way you can help, by letting her see that.'

That evening Marie whisked up big bowls of butterscotch Angel Delight for dessert, and I sat outside on the kitchen step watching the girls spin red Hula-Hoops with their skinny, hipless bodies. I felt numb and distant, hollow inside, worrying about what was happening to Mummy. When I heard the tap in the kitchen go and turned to see her there at the sink pouring a glass of water, I knew I had to show her I was all right. I began singing out the scores along with the girls, clapping and laughing loudly as Jennifer's hoop wobbled down onto the crazy paving, cheering Stella on; getting up, taking Jennifer's hoop and saying, 'My turn now. Show me how to do it, Jen.' Hoping Mummy could hear me – me being all right – me pretending everything was normal.

* * *

Abandoned

As the summer went by the girls became restless. Nobody, not even they, talked about my uncle, but they said they missed their friends and Michael and Liam who were still in London, and started to ask Mummy more often when we were going home. Kathy came over again and slowly Mummy pulled herself out of it. She started to drink less and did jigsaws with the girls on the dining room table; she polished her shoes and went into Marie's hairdressers in the precinct to have a perm. But when she had to talk to me, she still seemed to stare between my eyes, not at them.

The girls needed to get back to school and the boys needed their mum. I was outnumbered.

One morning she just left.

Chapter 26

The night before, when she told me she was going, I couldn't look at her. I was upstairs on Marie's bed watching TV with Stella and Jennifer. Mummy told the girls to go downstairs, that she wanted to talk to me on my own for a second. Stella took her time, picking playing cards up one by one and doubling the elastic band around the pack, saying she just wanted to watch the end of something. Someone opened the kitchen door downstairs and I heard the washing machine, suddenly realising it had been going all day. For some reason it made me glance up at the top of Marie's wardrobe and I saw that the blue leather suitcases had gone.

'It's for the best,' Mummy said.

She told me that Kathy and Brendan were looking for a boarding school for me to go to. She told me that I'd live at school and in the holidays I'd be able to come back to Marie and Peter's to stay.

I could see our tiny reflections in the blank TV screen up on Marie's dressing table. 'Please don't leave me, Mum, please. You said you never would ...' I felt childish saying it, but it just came out, the way I used to say it as a little girl. 'You've always said I'd never have to leave you.'

'Don't cry,' she said. 'You're making me cry again. You don't want that, do you?'

I shook my head.

'Look at me,' she said.

But I couldn't. I was frightened of what she might see in my eyes – what accusations might be there. I couldn't upset Mummy; I'd done enough already.

I said sorry over and over. 'What have I done?' I asked, finally.

She wiped her eyes on her sleeve. 'Nothing … Don't ever let me hear you say that, okay? You're as good as gold.' Saying it the way she used to always say it to me as a little girl. 'I don't want you thinking that.' She looked away, out at the trees at the back of the garden. 'It's for the best,' she said again. When her eyes swung back, they were dull and heavy, and something was missing from them.

'Don't let me down, will you? Let's just forget all this now; we don't need to talk about it again. Not to anyone …'

I knew she meant to Kathy and Brendan. I nodded, swallowing back tears.

'It's over now, okay?' she said. 'I'll always be your mum though, okay?' She pulled me towards her. I felt her tears wet against my face, and bit the flesh on the inside of my cheek, trying to hold back the tears. 'Always,' she said, 'no matter what happens, okay?'

All my life she had promised me no one would ever take me away from her, and now my whole family was being amputated overnight, just at a time when I needed them most.

* * *

Abandoned

The day Mummy left, something inside me snapped shut forever.

Kathy and Brendan stepped uneasily into the role of 'parents' after that. Brendan was like a real uncle to us by then, not just a family friend. Both of them still lived in Ireland and could only get over five or six times a year so there was only so much they could do. But there was nobody else to do it. Everything that had happened was pushed under the carpet. Maybe Mummy told the authorities that I was taken back over to Ireland to live with my 'real' mum; perhaps she told the police they just took me out of the country and she didn't know where I was. Maybe that was why no social workers were involved.

Brendan and Kathy arranged for me to go to boarding school. To begin with I was so desolate without Mummy and the rest of my family that I didn't care what happened to me. All I knew was that I had lost the one person I needed most. I didn't have a family or a home any more. My worst fears had come true. It felt like I was being punished for what I'd done. But I soon found that boarding school was the perfect place to try to forget your past.

On the outside I adapted easily and rapidly: sleeping in dormitories was like being at home with all my brothers and sisters again, but with nobody to bully me or tell me I was different. Here everyone was different, and everyone had a different surname, not just me. And adapting to a new life in such a different environment, with all the strict rules and new ways of doing things, left me little time to think about the past. It was like brainwashing and I loved it.

On the inside everything was being gradually shrink-wrapped, stored out of sight. There was never a time I forgot my earlier life: the abuse and the violence, and how it all ended. It didn't go away. It was all bound together in my mind with the separation from Mummy, and I couldn't forget her. But the memories and the painful feelings soon pulled away from each other, like skin from bone. I would think of what had happened in the past sometimes, but without feeling. At other times, not thinking of anything at all, I would suddenly feel things for no reason, stopped in my tracks with emotions I didn't understand.

I was surprised how quickly I adapted to boarding school and absorbed all the new ways of doing things. I had elocution lessons and riding lessons and started to do well in class, and gradually came out of my shell and settled in well. Everyone was surprised that I didn't feel homesick, but then there was no home for me to be home-sick for. Kathy was still living at home caring for her elderly father over in Ireland, who still didn't know about me, and Brendan had his own family, so even on my many trips over there during the holidays I couldn't be a part of their families or stay in their homes, as I had once stayed at Brendan's house for a holiday as a child. I did phone Brendan on his home number sometimes, and they encouraged me to write letters to them, but I always had to send them to their business address.

It was Mummy's letters I longed for. She was never much of a letter-writer and they only came occasionally. When they did arrive I soon found myself embarrassed at her spelling mistakes, and even at the cheap blue writing paper. I was ashamed of myself for noticing that, but I'd become accustomed to the expensive cream paper my friends' letters were written on and the type I now used in the expensive leather writing case Brendan bought me.

Abandoned

When the other girls got their letters and parcels from home handed out in the long, oak-panelled dining room during breakfast, memories of Mummy and my old home would come up and I would yawn them away, trying hard not to see the flashes of long blonde hair, just like Stella's and Jennifer's, amongst all the younger girls who were darting between the tables handing out the post. None of my friends knew I had any brothers and sisters. 'They'll only ask you why they don't go to boarding school too,' Kathy and Brendan told me. 'Just say you don't have any.' So I did.

When Mummy's letters did arrive I would never hand them around the table or read parts aloud in the dormitory as some of my friends did. I read them quickly, trying to conceal the thin, cheap envelopes they came in, and mention of the brothers and sisters I wasn't supposed to have. As soon as I'd read them I'd stuff them into my pocket, later sliding them into one of Brendan's shirt boxes that I kept at the bottom of my tuck box, until I was alone and could read them through again. I was always left longing for more news and for something I couldn't have any more; and struggling with emotions I didn't understand.

The hardest times were the holidays and half-term breaks. All my friends grew more and more excited as they approached, but I came to dread them. For the first week or so I would stay with Brendan or Kathy in one of the big London hotels – the ones in which I had visited Brendan so shyly as a child – and then be put on a train down to Marie and Peter's for the rest of the holiday. Staying in all

Abandoned

the best hotels sounded exotic to my friends at school, but to me it was soon boring and lonely. All I really wanted was to go back to a proper home and family life like them.

Chapter 27

Nothing had ever felt secure in my life and I found it hard to believe that I would ever be safe from my uncle. Nobody ever told me what happened to him, so I could only hope that he was in prison.

Although I was surrounded by people at school I felt very alone whenever the fear struck. When I woke at night from unsettling dreams or my one recurring nightmare, or when I doubled over with sudden stomach cramps during the day or woke in the mornings soaked to the armpits in warm urine, there was no one to talk to about it, no one to help me understand the emotions. So I shut them down more and more. I taught myself not to feel things.

The nightmare I had for years afterwards was always the same in every detail. It was me at a railway station, about to board a train. Mummy was with me on the platform, seeing me off, but just as I stepped up onto the train my uncle appeared and tried to pull me from the carriage. She tried to fight him off, screaming, just like she used to in real life, both of us crying, terrified. He dragged me out onto the platform and they pulled me in different directions, one by the arms, the other by my legs. They pulled so hard I was ripped apart, blood and guts spilling out, my intestines and organs left in a bloody pile on the platform. I was still not dead though. I was lying there watching it all, until finally the two of them just laughed and walked away together, arm in arm.

When my friends came up to my bunk and tried to comfort me, asking me what the nightmare was, I'd say I couldn't remember, or make up other ones to tell them.

I spent most of my life covering up my background, shrugging it off, trying not to think about Mummy and my brothers and sisters and what happened back at home. The other girls in my dormitory Blu-Tacked their family photos beside their beds. When, at night, they drew their fingers across them, saying 'Love you' and pressing finger-kisses down on smiling faces, I looked away, finding some distraction, blinking images of Mummy, Stella, Jennifer and the boys out of my head. They'd gone now; that life was over.

Chapter 28

Although I saw Brendan only four or five times a year, he was the closest thing I had in my life to a family now. I still had no idea who my real father was, so my relationship with him was in many ways like that of father and daughter.

His visits gave me a taste of what it would be like to have a family, but never the real thing. When he left I always felt more alone than before. Sometimes, when he and Kathy turned up to collect me from school together, introducing themselves as my 'parents', and we stayed in hotels in London, sleeping in a big triple room and going out to dinner and the theatre every evening, it felt like we were a proper family. But of course we weren't; they both had their own lives and families over in Ireland. So as much as I enjoyed our time together, even if I pretended I didn't, I always knew it would be over too quickly and never allowed myself, or them, to get too close.

It was particularly hard to accept Kathy's new role in my life. I didn't need another mum, and couldn't let her in I felt that they were just hiding me away in boarding school because I had to be kept a secret, in case the affair Kathy had had came out. Sometimes the loneliness I felt deep down would surface. And, as I grew more confident,

Abandoned

I would challenge them on the decisions they had made about me, complaining that I didn't fit in anywhere now.

'What were we supposed to do, send you to a home?'

'At least I'd belong to someone then. At least I'd be with other people who were the same as me. I'd learn to survive. They might not have families, but they've got each other; I've got no one. You've made me a freak. I don't fit in anywhere.'

'Of course you do.'

'Where?'

'You'll find your place. Wait until you're qualified then you'll see,' Brendan would always say. 'You'll be one of them then, with your own people. No one will care where you come from then.'

'I'll care,' I'd always snap before storming off to the bathroom or turning up the volume on my Walkman.

'Qualified' was Brendan's magic word, as if my becoming qualified at something would some day make everything okay.

Only with Brendan was I nearly myself. I opened up to him in a way I didn't with others. Some of the time he seemed to understand me but I still wasn't used to the intensity of the attention he aimed at me for those few days, a few times a year. I could never allow myself to open up fully, or get too close, because at the end of those few days he would be gone, back to his own family in Ireland.

It was the same with Kathy. Just as I was starting to feel close to them they would leave, off on a plane over to their own lives. They were always leaving. So I never risked showing them I needed or liked them.

Abandoned

Apart from Peter, who I didn't see that much of, Brendan was the only male role model in my life, the only one to show me that not all men were as bad as my uncle had been, that not all of them had to be feared, the way I still feared him. As his business did well over in Ireland, he tried to make up for what had happened and the family life I was missing out on by throwing money at me. I always had the best-quality things at school and more pocket money than most of my friends and they were all impressed at how much my uncle Brendan 'spoilt' me. But expensive possessions could never replace the things I really needed.

I was often at the outer edges of truth when talking to other people about my family. I didn't flesh out the lies, but I implied them: 'My Mum chose it,' I'd say about some article of clothing or present I'd bought myself with the money Brendan or Kathy gave me. 'My Mum gave it to me.' 'It used to be my Mum's …'

'My Mum', the best sound in the world, wrapping it around myself, like a big circle of love.

Chapter 29

It was almost a year before I saw Mummy again. But when she came through the revolving doors of the hotel to meet us that first time, and her face lit up in a smile when she saw us, it was as if nothing had changed. I was trying to be grown-up in my first pair of court shoes, but ran across the lobby to give her a big hug, crying into her hair when she told me how much they'd all missed me.

Once every school holiday after that she'd meet us somewhere for tea. Seeing her for just those couple of hours would rip me open afresh each time, but there was no way I could put those feelings into words to anyone.

Once, when she came to have tea with Kathy and me, I remember being struck by how strangely out of place and ill at ease she looked in the hotel dining room, pretending too hard that she wasn't. She sat there chain-smoking, smelling the milk to see if it was off, fidgeting while we finished eating. She checked her watch against one of ours, saying, 'Is that the time already? That can't be right,' shaking her wrist and pressing her watch to her ear before gulping back the last of her tea and leaving us all with a smile as she complained, as usual, at the 'daylight robbery' of the sandwiches. Reapplying orangey-pink lipstick and tying a quick, loose knot back into her neckscarf, she tutted loudly as Kathy piled money onto the silver dish and handed it up to the waiter.

Kathy and I had smiled, half-embarrassed, as Mummy pulled one of the sandwiches apart, not caring who saw or overheard her, shaking her head at the scrape of butter, the soggy slivers of cucumber clinging to the top slice, the 'mean little strips of pink ham'.

'That wouldn't have cost a fraction of the price to make. Don't leave a tip, they've made enough money out of you already,' she said, pressing the triangles of bread back together again and tossing it back onto the plate. 'They saw you coming.'

I laughed nervously, delighted at her outspokenness, but the loudness of my laughter made up for how suddenly embarrassed I was in case the waiter overheard her, and then for how ashamed I was of myself for seeing her differently in this setting. I hoped the waiter hadn't noticed the chipped nail varnish or the yellow nicotine stains on her fingers, or the dull frizz of her outgrown perm, rusty at the ends, or the quality of her clothes – all of which I was seeing for the first time. I felt a blush splash across my face and lowered my eyes, feeling disloyal, hoping she hadn't guessed what I was thinking.

Whenever Kathy and Brendan came over they were impressed with all the changes in me, but Mummy seemed uncomfortable with them. Although I couldn't have put words to it then, I was beginning to see that what all this time away at school was teaching me most was the differ-ence between Mummy and Kathy, and to be ashamed of the way I used to live. I was sitting between worlds, my elocution lessons and privileged schooling turning me into someone different.

I watched Kathy dab her lips with her napkin and the waiter smile flirtatiously with her as he passed. Mummy patted her double chins saying, 'Well, when you get to my age …' and Kathy and I smiled and exchanged a look which I wasn't certain I understood, or meant.

'I haven't got time for all the lotions and potions like my sister,' Mummy said, winking at me, and half-memories of the times she used to say that to me after all the arguments came up like slow air bubbles through mud. I forced a smile and told Mummy she looked great. I couldn't look in Kathy's direction, and suddenly her voice annoyed me. I looked down at their cigarette butts in the ashtray, reminding myself that I preferred Mummy's, smeared with her orangey-pink lipstick. The pain, like a lump of ice, stuck in my chest.

Chapter 30

When I eventually found out who my father was I was fourteen years old. I was sitting cross-legged on a bed opposite Kathy in the Savoy hotel, and had been guessing. Until then I'd been told me that my father was dead, but as I got older I wanted more information than that, wanted to piece my identity together. And for some reason she finally decided to tell me the truth.

She told me he wasn't dead, but that she had been waiting until I was old enough to understand.

'He wants to meet you,' she said.

'When?'

'He'll be joining us on Monday,' she said.

Thoughts were going through my mind so quickly I could hardly process them. I suppressed a nervous laugh and stared at her, trying to guess her feelings. But when it came to emotions, Kathy had always been as unfathomable as I was; I had no idea what she was thinking. I watched her place her cup back on its saucer, and dab her lips with the corner of the linen napkin spread across her lap. Everything she did seemed to be for an audience, a bit unnatural – 'all show', I heard my uncle's voice say loudly in my head. I blinked it away, but his words brought back memories my mind had been trying to bury for years, and particularly of all those times he had wanted to know who my father was.

She wasn't pushing me for a response and I still didn't have one. I just felt flat. Dozens of questions came into my mind, but none would settle. I couldn't believe that my father was alive and I was finally going to find out who he was.

'He'll join us on Monday,' she'd said, saying it in a way that made us sound like a family: a mother and daughter waiting for Daddy to arrive home for supper.

She wouldn't tell me who he was, though, or anything else about him. She said they had decided to wait until Monday, to tell me together. It felt like they were almost treating it as a game; him letting her break the news first, expecting me to wait a whole weekend until we went to Heathrow to meet him, saying she'd promised him she wouldn't tell.

'We agreed,' she said, leaning back on the bed on her elbows and smiling warmly. I couldn't bear the suspense or understand the reason for it. One bombshell was enough. I wanted to know who my father was before he arrived so I could prepare a reaction. Kathy was evidently enjoying the game of happy families she was playing. She seemed to relax and her face lit up in a way I hadn't seen before. We were suddenly a family unit and she looked like the cat who had finally got the cream.

I soon fell into the new role, becoming intrigued and more and more excited at the prospect of being part of someone's family again – replacing Kathy in my mind with Mummy, of course. All evening I plied her with questions about him. It was fun for both of us for a while. I sat guessing aloud who he could be, becoming more and more outrageous with my suggestions and the questions I asked to narrow him down. When she told me that he was looking forward to meeting me at last I giggled nervously, feeling everything at once.

'Is he?' I asked, smearing Vaseline on my lips, and trying to show I wasn't that concerned.

'Of course. He loves you.'

It was hard to imagine being the focus of someone's love all those years and not knowing about it.

I'd already wrestled some information from her: I knew he was Irish, and her strained expression when I asked told me that I had already met him on one of my visits. I tried to recall all the Irishmen I'd ever met, calling out half-remembered names or descriptions randomly, groaning into the pillow as I considered the awfulness of some of the possibilities. Kathy's usual reserve around me fell away too, and her laughter seemed easy and genuine; the way she laughed with everyone else.

I decided to be more systematic, to work out who he was by a process of elimination. I started by ruling out Brendan.

'It isn't him, is it?' I said.

It wasn't really a question. I said it dismissing him, as my mind raced on searching my memory for other men it might have been. Brendan had already told me it wasn't him anyhow. Driving alongside the canal on the way back to school at the start of the summer term the year before, I'd asked him out of the blue if he was my father. I didn't dare look at him, staring out at the long chain of barges roped to the sides of the canal as we passed.

When he said that he wasn't I blushed, remembering all the times as a little girl that I had secretly wanted it to be him. Anyway, if it had been Brendan, Mummy would have known. Eventually she would have given in and told my uncle during all those years he was convinced it was Brendan, rather than go through all those arguments, all that drunken rage and violence. Much as she loved her younger sister, and would have wanted to keep her secrets and protect her, she wouldn't have gone through all that if she could simply have told him who the father was. Also, she was my mother by then and no mother would have let her child endure all that name-calling and fighting. It would have broken her heart to watch her child suffering like that. She would have screamed it out as loudly as she could. Eventually.

I saw Kathy's face flood with colour when I said that it wasn't Brendan. Although there was hardly any change of expression and her eyes were downcast, she was clearly agitated, unconsciously twirling the ring on her finger. Waves of panic rolled through me as I watched the flush work its way up her neck and spread across her face, and she must have seen the colour drain from mine. I felt my whole past rearrange itself in a flash.

'It's not … is it?' I asked, desperate for the answer to be no, but reading a yes from her face even before she finally nodded.

A stampede of memories came into my head: twelve years of fists and screaming and all-night arguments. A whole childhood of Mummy answering in a thousand ways that 'Honest to God … I swear on my father's life,' she didn't know who Kathy's 'fancy-man' was, 'but I know for a fact that it's not Brendan Walsh.'

As the years had gone by, and I came to like Brendan more and more, I felt disappointed that it wasn't him. He was always so different from the other men in our lives: gentle and kind and sensitive. But he was always Mummy's weapon of last resort too. She had threatened my uncle so many times that Brendan was involved in the IRA (though of course he wasn't), and that one phone call from her 'was all it would take'.

'All it would take for *what?*' my uncle would scream. Then the insults and obscenities he kept exclusively for Brendan would begin, the special lexicon of hate he reserved for him unleashed like furies around our front room.

'Why are you lying for them?' he'd roar. 'Tell me who the father is, or their bastard is out,' he'd say, leaping over to punch me for crying. And all the time it had been Brendan.

'Did Mummy know?' I finally asked, getting it out at last.

She looked almost surprised by the question. She still had no idea exactly how much trouble she had caused by flitting in and out of our house and our lives over the years.

'Yes,' she said, quietly, but with no real sense of apology. 'Mummy always knew.'

I couldn't have said whether I felt angry or shocked or betrayed. Nothing made sense. Not anything. Why wouldn't Mummy have told my uncle if she knew? Kathy couldn't have realised how important it was for me to know whether Mummy had known. The thought that Kathy and Brendan had been having an affair all the time, betraying his wife and daughters, shocked and appalled me. I had truly but naively chosen to believe over the years that they were just good friends – him helping her out because she never had anyone else. I even felt guilty, that I was some-how implicated in the whole deception now. But the fact that Mummy knew who my father was all along, yet kept her sister's secret for her all those years, stunned me.

I couldn't speak, no words came out. I just broke down in floods of tears. Over and over I heard Kathy asking me what was wrong and why I was crying, and please could I tell her what I was thinking – but her voice came from somewhere far away and I couldn't respond. I wanted to, and I wanted to stop crying. I was nauseous and exhausted from it; my head was pounding but inside it was numb. All I could think was what Mummy had been put through all those years because of me being there, just because they forced her to lie about Brendan in order to protect themselves. They could have helped her so much by telling my uncle the truth.

Kathy came and sat on the edge of the bed and put her arm across my shoulders. I tensed under her touch, feeling her rings through the thin wool of my sweater as she slowly rubbed my back. I had longed for somebody's touch all those years but I shrugged her away and cradled my head in my hands. I had the kind of headache I'd had as a child, like all the bones of my skull were being crushed, my brain squeezed to the size and tightness of a fist.

She crossed to the bathroom. I heard the screech of the taps and water gushing into the hand basin and then the swish of her skirt coming back towards me. 'Here,' she said, taking my hand and lifting it up to a cold, wet flan-nel. Her touch was so light. 'I wish you would tell me what you're thinking … This is difficult for me … Is it good, or bad? Just nod.'

I wanted to tell her all the things we'd gone through with my uncle because they wouldn't tell him who my father was, but I couldn't. In my head I heard Mummy say, 'Don't tell her, I don't want them looking down on me.' So I didn't, because I didn't want that either.

Kathy lit another cigarette and tried to phone Brendan. 'You're frightening me,' she said. 'I don't know what you might do.'

I went and locked myself in the bathroom. When I came out several hours later I felt so light-headed and weak that I could hardly walk to the bed. Even the blankets touching my head hurt. Kathy was already curled in the other bed next to me with the lights off and her back turned. Once I was in bed she told me in a small, shaky voice that she had phoned Brendan and he would be coming over the following morning now instead. She was scared of being alone with me; but it was me who was most scared. Why couldn't they see that?

Chapter 31

The next day we went to Heathrow to meet him. I hadn't wanted to go but Kathy insisted. I trailed reluctantly through the airport behind her, feeling tense and nauseous and ashamed of them both.

Brendan hardly changed over the years. He came through Arrivals with his long, loose stride, wearing his winter coat open over his pinstriped suit and swinging his overnight bag. He looked the same as I remember him walking along the landing of our flats all those years ago, tall and athletic. But this time he was grinning sheepishly, making him look more boyish than ever. My eyes welled up again and I wanted to run in the opposite direction. I felt so deceived by them both.

I also felt a bit disappointed to find out that my father was 'just' Brendan, having fantasised about who else it might have been most of my life. He walked over to say hello, putting out his hand to touch mine, but I shoved both hands into the pockets of my duffle coat and looked away. There was a long, awkward silence, the three of us just standing there as around us 'normal' families talked and laughed and flung their arms around each other. He gave Kathy a peck on the cheek for the first time ever in front of me and I turned away, embarrassed in case anyone knew they were having an affair. I felt like I was intruding on something now; I felt even more shut out.

Brendan started writing me long letters at school to win me around, one every fortnight. I pushed them down under the waistband of my skirt and read them upstairs in my room later, humiliated in case any of my friends saw them. The letters explained how they had met and everything that had happened, how much they had tried to stay apart and how much they both cared for me.

They stayed with me together more often after that, keen to explain things to me and to give me a bit of 'proper' family life now I knew Brendan was my real father. It seemed a relief to both of them to talk about their affair with me. And knowing that I was one of the few people they could talk to about it made me feel valued in a strange way, and in some ways it brought us closer – although, as a teenager, I was still ashamed of them for it, especially since I knew Brendan's wife and children.

They'd still arrive at hotels and leave a few days apart so they weren't seen on the same flights. And Kathy would still hide in the bathroom when room service arrived so they weren't seen in the room together in case the waiter or waitress was from Ireland and somehow knew them. But at least now I understood why.

'It was true love. We tried to stay apart, but sometimes when a love like that comes along ...' Kathy said defensively, but almost dreamily, sitting prim and upright on the edge of the bed, picking at her room service meal as Brendan admired her every move. She was telling him more than me, both of them animated now that I knew who he was, unused to having anyone to tell their secret love to and enjoying having an audience for it.

I should have realised Brendan was my father; I resembled him in so many ways. His colouring was different to mine and I didn't have his height or his heavy splattering of freckles, but behind them you could see me there. Our natures were very similar too. But no one ever mentioned the resemblance between us growing up, except Brendan himself occasionally. One day on the way to Hyde Park in a black taxi, he lifted my hand as I sat with him. He unclenched it gently, finger by finger, as my body tensed, and laid it palm to palm on his to measure it. My hot and clammy hand was half the size of his then but undeniably his in miniature – the same shape and proportions, the same narrow wrists and long, almost evenly-sized fingers – but at the time I didn't think that meant he was related to me.

I had imagined things would change completely once I knew who my father was, but they didn't. Especially now that it turned out to be Brendan. At times I could convince myself that my relationship with him and Kathy, and our playing 'happy families' in hotel rooms for a few days at each end of my school holidays, was 'normal' family life, but in truth I knew that it wasn't

He made an effort to get closer to me, giving me lots of attention, and now that I knew he was my father the promises piled up. He even talked about getting a 'family' home for us to live in one day.

But inside I still felt like I didn't belong anywhere. Even though Brendan said I could rely on him I knew I couldn't, that his family and his own children – who could never know about me – would always come first.

Even before I found out who my father was, I had always known my existence was awkward for everyone. Eventually that feeling became too much, and almost two years later I decided everyone would be better off if I wasn't around. I decided to end everything once and for all. I locked myself in the big, cold bathroom on the laundry corridor at school, the 'haunted' bathroom that everybody tried to avoid, and cut my wrist several times with a razor blade. Slumped there on the white painted floor, watching the blood spurt across the white planks, I completely expected and hoped to die. I'd taken painkillers beforehand and had a flannel in my mouth to muffle the screams, but the pain was excruciating and I couldn't cut deep enough.

Eventually, when someone rapped at the door asking me how long I was going to be, I asked them to use another bathroom. But they kept coming back. When they had gone another time I knew I somehow had to get back to the dorm before someone discovered me and sent for an ambulance, which would prevent me from dying. I tightened my school tie around my wrist just above the cut, pulling it as tight as I could with my teeth and other hand, cleaned up as best I could and bundled several hand towels around it. The lights were already out and everyone was asleep and I lay in bed with the towels wrapped around my arm soaked in blood, expecting to fall into a coma and not wake up next morning. But I did. The bleeding had stopped. Although the gashes were pretty messy for a long time, with a lot of effort I managed to conceal it all.

Things were even more unsettled after that. I felt more self-conscious and ashamed. It was another secret to hide, another incident to alienate me. I withdrew from my friends more and more – I didn't need *anyone*, I told myself.

That half-term Brendan was meant to meet me from the train, but he wasn't at the station. He was never reliable, always turning up late and breathless or getting arrangements wrong. We weren't allowed to leave without someone meeting us, but eventually I slipped away from whoever was chaperoning us and waited all day on the spot where I had agreed to meet him if ever that happened. I was feeling on the outside of everything, watching everyone meeting and greeting around me. He was supposed to be there at 11 a.m. I phoned his home number and his wife said she didn't know when he would be back, that he was away on business for a few days. I felt like telling her that I was the 'business', but of course I didn't. Hour after hour passed and I stood there at the station until 11 o'clock that night, ridiculously thinking that maybe he thought we were meeting at 11 p.m. rather than in the morning. Finally I went to the station police and a policewoman phoned the school for me.

She tried to chat to me, asking me about my family and what they did, and if I had any brothers and sisters, but every question felt like a trap and I shrugged most of them off. I had to censor everything, hold back, unable to be myself. I couldn't tell anybody I had brothers and sisters because it would have seemed odd if I was the only one who went to boarding school. Even my best friends at school had never known. I couldn't tell her where my 'parents' lived in Ireland either, or give her a telephone number to call either of them at home, in case Brendan's wife answered, or Kathy's father. Nobody was supposed to know about me. I was a secret.

I knew my silence made people feel uncomfortable, but it was easier to tell them nothing than tell them the lies and half-truths I was supposed to. Most of my life was a secret now – nobody at school was allowed to know about my 'past life' with Mummy and all my brothers and sisters. But if Mummy had had a telephone number I probably would have given her that, but she still didn't have a phone then.

Although I had already missed my last connecting train, they arranged for me to go back on the last train part-way, and for a taxi to meet me and drive me all the way through the foggy countryside to school. It was well past midnight when I got there and I felt stiff and cold and sleepy. I decided to have a hot shower to warm myself up. I didn't hear Matron coming until she ripped the shower curtain open angrily, demanding to know why I was having a shower at that time of night.

'What were you doing all day at the station?' she asked, her thin lips trembling with anger.

'Waiting,' I said, wrapping my arms around my dripping body, ashamed to be seen naked. It was only years later that I realised what conclusion she must have jumped to and why she was so angry.

I spent the rest of the half-term at school with the over-seas girls who had no one in Britain to go to either. It was a small school, so they were all my friends and we had a nice time, but I still felt left out, lonely and intensely aware I was a burden to Kathy and Brendan.

Everybody else just got on with things, so I did too; I knew my feelings must be wrong, so I pushed them further and further down. I withdrew more and more and felt alienated, certain that nobody could understand me, and by the end of the year I felt I didn't fit in at school either.

Staying with Kathy and Brendan in another hotel room, this time the Sheraton Skyline at Heathrow, I decided to tell them I wasn't going back the following term; that I wasn't going to school again, anywhere. There was no one to force me to. What could they do? They behaved like parents only when it suited them. I knew they'd be angry because the last thing they would want was the authorities getting involved.

I leaned back against the radiator in the hotel room telling Brendan of my decision. I felt almost detached, curious about what he would do as much as anything else. Deep down I wanted him to force me to go back, to take charge like a parent should if he really cared about me.

Brendan told me how selfish and ungrateful I was. That afternoon he stormed back to Ireland early and I was left wandering around Heathrow pretending there was nothing wrong. I'd wanted to be able to speak my mind, to shout and scream and tell him that I didn't want him there, but I didn't want him to actually walk away and leave me. I could never have told anyone that, though.

Marie and Peter let me stay at their house, even though they had two children by then and Marie was heavily pregnant with their third. There were only three bedrooms, and since I was in one, all three of her children had to share one room. Nobody said I wasn't welcome, but once I was living there full-time I felt in the way. In the end I realised I had to go back to school but they had already told my headmistress I wasn't going back, so for a term I went to the local girls' comprehensive. It was a shock to the system after all those years at boarding school, and because of the time I'd missed I got moved back a year. I was soon bored with the classes and never made friends or settled in there.

No matter how kind Marie and Peter were and how lovely their house was, it never felt like a home I could really call my own. Brendan was paying them for my keep and I felt like a lodger, and still had this sense of longing for something I almost didn't recognise any more.

Chapter 32

When I was almost seventeen, five and a half years after I was whisked away to Marie's from the police station, I went back to visit Mummy in the house in London. It was the first time I'd been allowed to go back, and a few days before Marie had sat me down and told me that my uncle was back living in the house. I swallowed back the lump in my throat, but other than that I felt numb. I pretended it was the most ordinary thing in the world, and that it didn't bother me in the slightest. But for days I had headaches that wouldn't go and although I didn't put it into words it felt a little like my recurring nightmare, when I saw him and Mummy walking away together, leaving me torn to pieces on the platform.

When I arrived he was up a stepladder, changing a light bulb in the dining room ceiling. I walked quickly past the doorway, blinking away some cold, painful feeling I didn't recognise, and down into the sizzling roast lamb smell of the kitchen. Mummy whispered to me to go back in to say hello to him. I did as she said, as if nothing had happened. He was bent almost double up on the ladder to avoid the ceiling, but still looked enormous, bringing all my physical fears rushing back.

Abandoned

I stepped forwards, all smiles, one hand behind my back still gripping the doorframe. I hoped he'd speak first, but he didn't. The doorbell went and everyone was streaming into the hallway saying hello, bundling me into the family. I felt shy and awkward at suddenly being the centre of things. I opened my mouth, but nothing came out.

'Hi,' I said eventually.

'All right, Anya?' he said and the ice was shattered. He'd never asked me in my whole life if I was all right. *Everything really had changed.* I nodded that I was and tried to push the fear out of my smile. He nodded and our eyes met for the first time in all those years, before we both quickly looked away. Even hearing his voice again after so many years was frightening. He seemed quieter, though, like something had gone out of him. What I would have given for a 'sorry', but for the first time I felt pity for him, unaccountably saddened to see him standing so awkwardly at the top of that ladder. And I took his quietness as some kind of apology.

'Good girl,' Mummy said, smiling, when I went through to the kitchen.

It was a hot day. The boys' friends were in and out drinking tea and eating biscuits; everyone was laughing and happy. The whole house bustled with people and sound, radios and TVs playing in every room, the cat prowling around the place, flicking her tail. After the silence of my little box room at Marie and Peter's it felt like heaven. This was my family; these were my brothers and sisters. I felt I belonged again; I was part of something.

The boys were allowed to smoke in the conservatory.

'Go on,' Mummy said, 'I know you like a sneaky smoke, just don't let me see you do it.'

Abandoned

It was all so warm and easy-going and, still after all those years, everyone and everything was so familiar that when it was time to leave I didn't want to. I wanted to go back.

Mummy explained that my uncle had begged her to take him back. The girls had begged her too, she said. I guess she didn't have much choice. The girls needed their dad – and it would have been hard for her to cope on her own with four children still at home. He was a 'reformed character', she said, he'd learnt his lesson, he'd never do anything like that again, and the girls told me he didn't drink half as much any more, and that they hardly rowed like they used to.

After playing netball against a wall at the top of the road during that first visit, the girls linked arms with me on the way back. We bought a Chinese takeaway on the high street, and the men from the garage at the top came out flirting.

'Who's your friend?' they asked the girls.

'She's not our friend,' they said. 'She's our sister.'

I was so proud I couldn't breathe. I was a sister, part of something again. I belonged.

Stella bounced the netball along the pavement on the way back. 'I wish you were back living with us,' she said. 'It was much better with you here.'

Someone wanted me! My sisters wanted me! And my soul floated back into my body.

* * *

Abandoned

That night I told Marie I wanted to move back to London. She asked Brendan, who said he'd talk to Kathy. Nobody seemed able to make decisions for me. Finally Brendan flew over to try to talk me out of it.

'Why would you want to go back there?' he asked. But in his heart he knew why. I'd talked to him more than anyone over the years, all those late nights in hotel rooms, and he knew how much I missed them all, how empty I felt inside. He kept trying to fill it with God, or 'Wait until you are qualified, it'll all be different then.' Eventually he gave in and said he would ask Mummy. Mummy said she'd have to talk it over with my uncle.

What if they didn't want me? But they did and it was all agreed. The money Brendan was paying Marie and Peter to look after me would now be paid to Mummy. A new bed was bought and arrangements were made.

On my first day back Mummy took me aside and said: 'I know he won't, but if ever he does anything to you again, you make sure you tell me, okay?' I nodded. 'Now, that's the last we'll mention about all that stuff, okay? The past is the past. Forgive and forget; that's my motto. Let bygones be bygones.' And that was the first and last time we ever spoke of it.

Although I longed to be back as part of the family, it was hard to suddenly be amongst people who shouted and swore after years of people who had been calm and quiet and considerate to one another. Quickly all the emotions from the past resurfaced, and soon became overwhelming. But I couldn't tell anyone. When it got too bad, I retreated into books, which distanced me further from the rest of the family because none of them read for pleasure or studied for exams. I was seen as an oddity for it and ridiculed. 'Anya's trying to be different again, thinking she's better than the rest of us.'

Learning came easily to me and I did well at school, but deep down my only real ambition was to be part of my family. All I wanted was to be accepted by them all, to fit in and have a family of my own again. So I sat on the same settee as my uncle and watched news items or programmes that referred to some form of child abuse and didn't blink. I just sat there trying not to move a muscle, keeping my breathing shallow while he drank beer and chewed peanuts noisily, making sounds or movements to draw attention to himself. Sometimes I thought I saw a smile on his lips, or that look in his eyes I'd seen in the car park behind the police station that day. Both of us knew that I hadn't forgotten, even if I tried to give the impression I had, and only the two of us knew the full horror of what had gone on over those years.

After a couple of months I found myself back in the role of scapegoat, in amongst the chaos of their arguments and his drunkenness, repeatedly told that I wasn't wanted again, that I was 'out of here'. The novelty of having an older teenage sister in the house soon wore off for Stella, and they all started telling me I was their slave, laughing that they had only wanted me back to do the housework. The sarcasm and hostility and put-downs restarted. I had never heard anybody speak like that in the years I'd been away and it was shocking.

Abandoned

When I lost my small, pink five-year diary from board-ing school, with its little gold key and all my school friends' addresses in the back, I felt I had lost my last connection with that time. My memories of school began to blur and it soon seemed like another lifetime ago. By contrast, everything that had happened before I was sent away sharpened and came back into focus.

One boiling hot day that summer, the girls were out in their swimming costumes in the garden. There had been a huge drunken row the night before and Mummy and I were in the kitchen getting the lunch ready. Out of the long kitchen window we watched the girls squirming in delight as my uncle jetted them with cold water from the hose, hopping from foot to foot screaming, their hair drip-ping, their swimming costumes stuck to their slim, straight bodies.

Suddenly I was embarrassed. I wanted them to cover up, to get away from him. I knew he had learned his lesson, and wouldn't ever do anything like that again – especially to Stella and Jennifer – but I didn't know where to look. I wasn't ready for the feeling of horror that came up. I looked away. Not daring to look at Mummy I beat the stuffing smooth, trying to ignore the hot sharp pain tangled in my stomach. The mocking look in his eye when he came in to get a beer shocked me. I was sure he knew what I was thinking.

Soon I was back into a routine of housework and ironing. The only place I could do my homework in the evenings was the kitchen table, so if I wanted it cleared after dinner I had to do it myself. I'd do all the washing-up first while they all just got up, leaving their plates on the table, and went off to the other room to watch TV. I felt stunned after the serenity of those years away but at least I was still there, still one of them, even though I was the cause of most of the arguing again.

I agreed with things just to avoid confrontation, eager to please, wanting to do anything to fit in and be one of them. I threw myself into homework at night until my uncle started turning off the light in the kitchen, not letting me finish. I would take it under the bed covers with a torch, but the girls would call him to get me to turn it off.

'Dad! Tell Anya ...' was all they had to say, and I would feel a pain tightening across the back of my head as I switched it off and dropped my book to the floor, still as terrified of him as I'd been as a little girl.

I knew I'd never be accepted as myself and be able to fit in. When the arguments got more frequent and more and more violent again I said I wanted to do my A levels in a year, to make up for the year I was behind because of the change of schools. I asked Brendan if I could do them at a private tutorial college on the other side of London because it was the only place you could do A levels in a year. I knew Brendan would agree and wouldn't let me travel all that way every day when I could be studying. He came over and rented me a flat close to the college. It was the perfect excuse to leave home again, bringing my big blue school trunk back up out of the cellar and getting a taxi on my own after everyone went off to work and school.

I moved out on a Friday. On Sunday it was Mother's Day and I went back for lunch and to give Mummy her present and card. By then the girls had already swapped rooms with Mummy and my uncle, going back to the smaller room. A third bed wouldn't fit in that room too, and as I walked in Liam and my uncle were carrying my mattress out to the garden. They were laughing, on their way out to throw it over the back fence to burn it. It all felt so final. I had been fooling myself all along. I would never belong there.

Chapter 33

I was always looking for proof that Brendan loved me. Although he always said he was closer to me than his other children, and loved me as much, I never trusted his words. So when I turned eighteen and he kicked up a fuss, saying I was too young to go on my first holiday with friends, I saw it as proof of how much he cared for me, and told my friends almost proudly that my Dad wouldn't let me go.

Instead, he and Kathy planned a 'family' holiday to America for the three of us. I'd been away with both of them before but never together, except when I visited them in Dublin – when I usually just transferred between their cars on country roads. This would be the first time the three of us had been abroad as a 'family', and I was really looking forward to it. I was feeling very close to both of them by then, but particularly Brendan, who spoiled me whenever he came over, and who Kathy said I had wrapped around my little finger.

A few weeks before we were due to go, during one of his visits to meet a client in London, Brendan came with me to Somerset House to get a copy of my birth certificate so I could apply for a new passport. He waited outside while I went in. As I stood in the queue I saw a notice on the wall saying that fathers of children registered illegitimately could put their names to the certificate retrospectively. I went back outside to find him and asked him, proudly but shyly, if he would come in and put his name on mine. He looked offended and became very angry.

'You don't need a signature to know I'm your father. I'm paying for our holiday, aren't I? And I'm the one paying for your flat and to go to university. Who else would pay out thousands of pounds like that?'

I was stunned. Everything always came down to money with Brendan, but I thought he'd know how important this was to me. It wasn't about the money but about how much I needed to be acknowledged by him, even though he could never do that publicly because of their affair. I tried to get him to look at me, but he wouldn't. He stood there stiffly, his face without expression, waiting for me to go back in.

I tried to convince myself that he didn't deserve to have his name on my birth certificate, in an effort to dull the pain of the disappointment. But as I was thinking it, 'Please,' escaped my lips. I felt like I was betraying myself, hearing myself say it again. I had said please when I first asked; now it felt like I was begging.

'No,' he said angrily. He turned and walked off fast down the Strand, leaving me crying and ashamed amongst the crowds of tourists filing past.

He obviously didn't trust even me, and for a second I understood some of what my uncle must have felt over the years when they didn't trust him enough to tell him who my father was. I remembered Brendan once telling me he thought my uncle might blackmail them if ever he knew. I was offended and angry that he might think that of me too. Especially after all those years at boarding school when I had to phone him at home to tell him my holiday dates and the times of the trains to meet me. I could so easily have told his wife or one of his children who I really was when they picked up the phone. But of course I never would.

'It's not to blackmail you with … if that's what you think,' I shouted after him down the Strand. 'It's to get a passport, not to get even.'

I went back to get the birth certificate feeling wretched; dragging the heavy book off the shelf and over to the table, shaking with hurt and anger. When I saw the diagonal line drawn in blue ink through the last box in my entry, and in crabbed handwriting, 'unknown' written in place of 'Father's name', it seemed more accurate than the truth. That afternoon I realised I definitely didn't know him as well as I thought I had all these years.

Next morning he apologised for not doing that for me. Brendan rarely apologised for anything. When I recall the way he came out of the hotel bathroom – his face half-covered in foam, his razor lifted and head hung, telling me that he was sorry – I knew it was sincere. I knew that it couldn't wait until he was finished shaving; that perhaps he couldn't look into his own eyes. I felt he was apologising for more than that too. I still feel such a pang of love for him when I remember how sad he looked that time that I could forgive him anything.

He went on to explain that although he obviously couldn't put me in his will he had already arranged to set aside some money for me in a separate deal that none of his family knew about. I knew he was trying to show that he did consider me his daughter, although he couldn't publicly admit it or treat me the same as them. But I didn't even want to talk about it. I hated thinking that one day Brendan wouldn't be there.

Chapter 34

After A levels I got into university to study law. I thought I'd finally moved on from the difficulties of my childhood. I made a new life for myself and did well; all the old pain folded away deep inside me. No one who met me would have guessed what lay in my past. I graduated with a good degree, passed my postgraduate exams at the College of Law in Guildford, had a series of interesting jobs, fell in love, went on holidays with friends and did all the things you'd expect of a twenty-something woman. It seemed that I had survived my childhood.

I was still in contact with Mummy and the family during this period, visiting occasionally at weekends and going over for Christmas. But as new husbands, wives and friends came into the family, my role in it seemed more and more awkward to explain, and I felt increasingly uncomfortable. In some ways I was consciously moving on, but I felt pushed out too. Obviously they needed to tell people a better version of our past, cleaning it up and removing unsavoury chunks, but it was hard to accept when I was one of them. They distanced me more and more, phoning each other but not me; inviting everyone but me to family occasions; keeping me an awkward stranger in front of the new members of the family. And although I knew she still loved me, even Mummy slowly turned her back to keep the past a secret, retreating further and further over the years until, when she and my uncle finally emigrated to Spain to live with Liam and his family, I had very little contact even with her.

A few years after I graduated, Kathy and Brendan's relationship finally ended too. Neither of them would tell me why or talk to me about it, which made it harder for me to accept. They couldn't understand why I needed to know. 'It's none of your business,' Kathy once told me when I asked her why she wouldn't tell me what had happened. When their affair ended she said she was unable to cope with the connection to Brendan, and that I was part of that. She said she'd get back in touch when she could, but she never did. I wanted to keep the connection so I still called her every so often – as often as I dared – but it was always the same. She wasn't ready yet. Eventually I lost hope and gave up. The rejection was too painful to keep trying.

I was still in touch with Brendan. But when one of his children found out about his affair, and about me, things became more difficult. She would put down the phone whenever I called, or he would put it down whenever she came into the room. Soon even he was turning his back to keep his family together, only phoning me in secret occasionally, which felt sordid and wrong.

I was becoming more and more isolated from everyone. But the shell I had built up around me over the years to stop the feelings was numbing a lot of the pain.

Then, more than a decade after I'd graduated, I fell into a relationship with a man called Craig.

Chapter 35

I never intended becoming involved with Craig. I had just come out of a very good five-year relationship with Neil, my only real partner until then, and although ending the relationship had been the right decision I was feeling raw and emotionally vulnerable.

To begin with Craig was the best friend anyone could have. Supportive, sensitive and full of good advice and the empathy that helped me in getting over the break-up with Neil. Maybe inevitably, the friendship developed into a more intimate one, even though he was almost twenty years older than me and I wasn't really sexually attracted to him. We were never equal partners; he was more like a father figure at the beginning, and I quickly became emotionally dependent in ways I hadn't expected.

Very soon the relationship became controlling. Over the couple of years that I knew him, he gradually turned more and more mentally abusive, until in the end my world was smashed to pieces.

I'd told him some of my background and it wasn't long before he was using it against me. He'd also convinced me by then that I shouldn't see any of my family, that they were continuing to punish me, making me their scapegoat; even that Mummy and Brendan didn't love me. Brendan had just been trying to silence me over the years, he said, and Mummy had only been doing a favour for her sister, not really caring about me at all. He was the only one who had probably *ever* loved me, he said. Of course I knew that wasn't true, but somehow it got me questioning everything and thinking all sorts of dark thoughts. It was too distressing to even think about in the end so I just drank more and more to try to blot it all out.

My self-esteem and confidence were soon so low it was easy to convince myself I didn't deserve anyone's love. I didn't even try to make contact with family or friends. I thought Craig was all I had. When he said he loved me, I didn't even think I deserved that, despite how he was being by then. But as soon as I dropped my barriers and allowed myself to get close he would say twisted things like how my uncle was 'all right'; that I should forgive him for all the stuff he'd done to me; that it wasn't really a crime; that most men liked little girls like that.

The abuse was so gradual that I hardly noticed it at first. As an adult I hadn't met anybody like my uncle, but the little girl in me was so used to being treated like that in the past that I almost accepted the way Craig became towards me. Craig was tall, thin and pale-skinned, but emotionally it was like meeting my uncle all over again. He cracked my shell right open; and all those emotions from my childhood came flooding back. Soon I wasn't sure if I was reacting to something Craig was doing or saying, or something my uncle had done to me all those years ago, or that I had witnessed him doing to Mummy. Everything became very muddled.

* * *

Abandoned

After seeing Mummy go through what she had, I vowed that I would never stay in any kind of abusive relationship. But once I was in the relationship with Craig I didn't know how to leave it. The worse he became, the worse I felt about myself rather than about him. It was classic abusive stuff, I suppose. I became so fragile, vulnerable and dependent – and used to him flying into rages at the slightest thing – that I was almost too frightened to leave him. I was so ashamed that I had ended up in an abusive situation. He turned everything around so I ended up thinking it was all my fault, and I would be the one apologising to him.

Quite early on in our relationship he told me that he'd had treatment for mental problems. But all that was in the past. I didn't see any evidence of it until it was too late. Besides, to my mind that just made him vulnerable, not dangerous. It was definitely not a reason for me to walk away from him, especially since we were only friends to begin with. Mental illness wasn't contagious, I knew that much about it, but I didn't know how serious his illness sometimes got, and how much it was going to affect me.

He would swing between being the best person in the world to be with and someone who was manipulative, vicious and controlled by voices in his head, blaming me for everything. I was soon under his spell, and tried to understand and change him, rather than leave him.

He never actually hit me; it was always mental abuse. But on one occasion towards the end, when I disagreed with him about something, he suddenly jumped on me, his hands around my throat, tighter and tighter until I was choking, staring back at him in absolute terror and confusion. He said he was going to kill me; and I really thought he was. All the breath went out of my body and, gasping for breath, something opened up in me. I started to tremble inside and I never really stopped.

When he finally let go, all those old fears I'd had as a little girl flooded through me. I was fearful of everything after that, and although I wouldn't admit it to myself, I was right back in the mindset of that little girl.

I should have walked out and never come back that time, but I didn't. He held me afterwards and I didn't know how to walk away from the need for that. I just wanted to belong somewhere and to be taken care of. I became more and more distressed and more and more exhausted and couldn't cope with doing the most ordinary things on my own. I was doing the bare minimum of work; the stress of it all got to me. Even my periods stopped.

Whenever I got close to telling him I wanted to end the relationship he would tell me he was doing it all on purpose to shake me up a bit; that I was like a stuck wristwatch; that he was doing it to get me moving, to start me up again. That made a kind of sense to me because deep down there was that bit of me that felt like that. I was beginning to feel so vulnerable and 'controlled' by him that by some perverse twist in my thinking I sometimes fell into believing that he was doing me some good after all.

Other times, when I felt stronger and threatened to end the relationship, he would tell me he'd end up in a mental hospital again if I ever left him. I felt it impossible to just walk away then, and he knew it; he had been manipulating and playing mind games with me right from the start. But in the end I did run away.

Abandoned

I moved flat twice and changed my telephone number, but he tracked me down each time and pleaded with me to come back. My head was so muddled by the end that even after I got away I would sometimes think the 'episodes' he went into were my fault for not loving him enough. When he said I could never get away from him, that his 'voices' would find me wherever I was and lead him to me, I was so freaked out and manipulated by him that I believed him, despite telling myself how ridiculous and impossible that was. I was frightened of my own shadow in the end.

I saw him one last time, on Tottenham Court Road. He came out of nowhere by a row of shops opposite Habitat as I waited at the bus stop one evening. His waxy face lit up like a pumpkin in the dark, terrifying me with his words: 'You'll come back to me because there'll be nowhere else for you to go. You don't belong anywhere, you never have. Neither do I. People who don't belong, belong to each other …' I stood up to get the bus and he was still whispering beside me, 'You'll come back to me. I'm the only one who will ever love you. You'll never get away.'

Sitting on the top deck with tears streaming down my face and his words crashing through my head, I was shaking uncontrollably, convinced he was sitting on the lower deck and would follow me to my new flat, and that I *would* never get away. I sat there until the end of the line, until the driver flashed the lights to tell me to get off. I had decided I had to go. I didn't know where. I just knew I had to get away from him and from London.

There was nothing left for me to stay for anyway. I was too ashamed to go back and tell any friends or even Mummy or Brendan the kind of relationship I had been in with Craig, or let them see how broken and shaky it had left me. I felt like such a failure. Both my best friends from university had recently left London almost at the same time – one to live in Germany, one in South Africa – but I hadn't been in touch with them for over two years anyway.

I handed in my notice and fled to Newcastle, where I was offered some temp work and rented another flat. But I was in too much mental turmoil to rebuild my life effectively. I fell into a depression that I didn't seem able to pull myself out of. Life seemed to be covered in a grey veil; I felt smothered by it and had little energy for anything at all. I felt lethargic and flat and shaky, and close to tears almost constantly. Work was soon drying up, leaving me struggling to make ends meet and taking out loans to pay bills. I was still waiting for my ex-partner, Neil, to repay some money I had put into his business. I had invested all the savings I had, but in the end it didn't save his business, and I knew he was still in real financial difficulties. It wasn't a legal agreement, but I'd never known him to go back on his word, so it felt realistic to think that he would still pay me back.

I'm not sure I was realistic about much else, though. I wasn't coping. Diagnosing me with clinical depression, the GP gave me a letter that I eventually used to sign on for social security. It felt like defeat, but I knew it would only be for a short while. It would take the pressure off me for a bit.

When the tenancy on my flat came to an end I knew I had to give it up, but I had no idea where to go next. I had no friends, no job and no idea what to do about it. Craig's words, after all this time, were still swirling about inside my head. I felt entirely alone.

Chapter 36

With my whole life falling apart around me, I was desperate to have someone around who I knew was on my side. So at Christmas I got back in touch with Brendan. Despite what Craig had been trying to convince me, I knew he must love me. I sent him my new mobile phone number on a Christmas card, and when I answered it one day and heard the sound of his voice I broke down in tears.

I hadn't intended letting him know how bad things had got, but I ended up telling him about Craig and why I had moved out of London, and about the depression that had set in.

All the emotion of the last two years came pouring out and we had the most tearful, emotional, father–daughter conversation I ever remember having with him. He was his old reassuring self and I felt like that little girl again, protected from the world by his warmth. At one point – I think only half-joking – he even offered to send someone over from Ireland to kill Craig. My father was standing up for me! I was overwhelmed. It was wonderful not to be alone any more.

I think this was what made me believe Brendan so easily when he told me again about the money he had intended to set aside for me since he couldn't include me in his will. He told me he could give it to me now instead, as there was a deal he was doing that none of his family knew about. The amount was a bit more than I had lent Neil, so I'd be able to pay off my debts and the loans I'd taken out, and also have enough for a breathing space so I could start putting my life back together.

At any other time I would have been more sceptical. But, totally exhausted, I just wanted someone else to take charge, to make decisions for me. And, despite how old I was by then, the thought of Brendan coming through for me, being the kind of father he had been to his other daughters, was something I so much wanted to happen.

Perhaps alarm bells should have rung when he soon told me there was a delay, that there was nothing he could do about it, and that I'd have to wait. He suggested I go away for a few weeks, 'Three or four, it definitely won't be longer than that.'

'How definite are you?' I asked, remembering all the times he'd let me down over the years, all the complicated ways he used to pay my school fees so that his family didn't find out, using deals they knew nothing about, deals that always seemed to go wrong, fall through or be delayed. 'You've said that before,' I reminded him.

'This time I am 99.9 per cent sure of it!'

He told me to wait a while before I made a decision about where to go next, encouraging me to have a rest and to wait until the money came through before I pinned myself down to living in a part of the country I might not want to be in.

Abandoned

In a way I wished I wasn't relying on him, but in the state I was in it was hard to walk away. It was as much about having my trust restored; knowing that 'my father' was coming through for me. I was giving up on life and he was taking care of me. He was my Dad, the only family in the world I had left, even though nobody could know about that. His suggestion I go away for a while was tempting – what I needed more than anything was a rest … a long, long rest so I could let down my guard and allow my scars to heal.

Looking back, what I should have done was use the last of my money and overdraft limit to get another tenancy and job in the area, or somewhere else outside London where rents were cheaper. But I no longer had the energy to pull my life together. It felt like one fight too many. Instead, I put my belongings in storage, loaded up the car and took Brendan's advice to have a break from everything.

I overloaded the car with boxes, suitcases and bags. I knew I would probably never even open most of them, but I wasn't sure when I would get my stuff out of storage, so I took far more than I needed. The thought of having no home to return to was scary, like jumping off a cliff, but I was convinced Brendan would come through for me this time.

I couldn't make even the simplest decisions: not even about where to go for those few weeks. Brendan reminded me of a holiday in north Norfolk I'd often told him about, and for want of any other ideas, on my last night in Newcastle I decided to head there.

Next day I signed the inventory of my flat with the lettings agent, handed the keys back and pulled the door firmly shut, having no idea that it would be more than eighteen months before I had another door of my own to lock behind me.

Chapter 37

That night, feeling tired and apprehensive at putting all my trust in Brendan again, I booked into a bed and breakfast by a windmill in one of the small coastal villages of north Norfolk. It was February and out of season, and at the tourist office the following morning I rented a cottage for a week near Holkham at a cheap rate. Utterly drained, I did nothing for the first few days but lie on the bed for hours on end, staring out at the sky and the huge, ravenous seagulls that circled noisily above. At night I lay in the dark, listening to the wind battering the building. I began to feel calmer and safer than I had for months, and when I discovered the cottage was empty for another week I extended my stay, curling up on the overstuffed pumpkin-coloured sofa downstairs, staring into nothing and planning how to put my life back together.

After three weeks I was feeling stronger than I had in ages. The depression was beginning to lift. But when Brendan called to tell me the deal was being held up again, my world seemed to collapse, and I was reminded of all those times he'd let me down in the past. What Craig had said about him kept coming into my head. But he sounded as dejected as I did and I knew he felt bad about letting me down. He said he was even more certain that the deal would come through now, and told me to sit tight, that it couldn't be more than another month or so. A month felt like an age away then. In the meantime, because he knew my money was about to run out, he arranged to help me out while I waited; he was able to send me some money every fortnight. It wasn't much, but together with running up credit card debt it would see me through if I did wait.

Sitting alone in that cottage in Norfolk I couldn't think straight. The last of the deposit the letting agents had refunded to my account was almost gone, and I wouldn't be able to get another bank loan now I wasn't working and without an address. Brendan wouldn't tell me much about the deal but he was still saying the money would definitely come through. 'It could be any day,' he said almost every time I phoned. In the end I simply didn't have the energy not to believe him.

What followed were the most barren months of my life. I decided to leave Norfolk but carry on waiting for another few weeks, trusting what Brendan was telling me. Depression had taken hold again and I couldn't think what else to do.

I had no energy for the simplest things, and ended up dragging myself from place to place around the country, waiting; living on credit in places I didn't want to be in. I slept a lot; sometimes for whole days. My life had absolutely no focus or purpose. Everything was 'on hold', even my emotions.

Week rolled into week and delay followed delay. Three months later I found myself still waiting: still travelling around the country, driving aimlessly up and down the motorways, staying in holiday homes, B & Bs and hotels everywhere from Carlisle to Cornwall, completely exhausted and lost. I felt if I could just reach out my arm and hold back time for a moment while I tried to make a decision, everything would be okay; but as it was I was disorientated and alienated, and overwhelmed by the smallest decisions. Sometimes, curled up in yet another bed at night, feeling like I'd never belong anywhere, Craig's words would come into my head – 'those who don't belong, belong to each other' – and I had to force myself not to think of going back to him. It would be utter madness, but this felt like madness too.

I've no idea what a doctor would have said about my condition. Was it a breakdown? Had my GP's diagnosis of clinical depression turned into something worse? All I know is that Brendan's promise that the deal was 'about to come through' dominated my mind, until hanging on to that belief was all that kept me going.

Eventually all the towns and villages began to look the same. I lost track of where I was. Late one evening at the end of a week staying in yet another rented place, driving to the garage for milk, I froze at the first main round-about, unable to remember which exit to take. I had driven that way every day for almost a week, but suddenly every roundabout and the directions to every garage in every town and village I had visited merged in my head. For a few blank minutes, I had no idea which place I was in.

My life was falling apart and I was not taking responsi-bility for it. Every morning I woke exhausted, feeling like I hadn't slept a wink. I never seemed to have enough energy to get me through the day. Depression was cloud-ing everything. I was living on credit and had turned my back on any support system that might have been there for me, telling myself it was a temporary blip, not realising it was about to become a landslide.

One day I found myself in the queue at the tollgates into Wales. I panicked, unable to decide whether to go through. Cars had pulled up behind me and soon it was impossible to reverse. A rusty, white camper van stalled in front of me, and in those few seconds I made the decision not to go through: Wales was too far from any possible ways out of my situation, it seemed at that moment. When I reached the booth I told the man that I was lost and hadn't intended going through.

'Where are you headed?' he asked.

My mind went blank. I wasn't headed anywhere.

'Glasgow,' I said. It was the only place far enough away from there that came to mind.

'Glasgow?' He raised both eyebrows and took off his glasses. 'You're a fair way from Glasgow here.'

He pushed his way noisily out of the booth and guided me importantly through the double row of orange cones and out onto a slip road that would take me around the back and then over the motorway bridge to join the traffic going north.

Instead, when I was sure my green Rover was out of sight, I looked for the route south and drove towards Bristol and then down to Brighton. I wasn't sure why, except that Brighton was close to London, so maybe I was feeling my way slowly back there. Craig might still be there but London was the place where the jobs and the opportunities were most likely to be, and the only place that had ever felt like home to me.

Abandoned

I knew Brighton a bit too. Brendan often used to drive me down there for days out when I was a child, and years later I used to meet friends from work on the beach for picnics after the London to Brighton cycle ride. I also liked it because it was a place where people came and went, a place where I could be anonymous while I continued to 'wait' – although I had almost forgotten what I was waiting for by that stage. I was just stuck in a week-by-week, dependent relationship with Brendan.

I liked the dilapidated grandeur of the big white Regency houses along the seafront too. It seemed to reflect my life and spirit, falling apart just like those buildings, or like the charred and ruined West Pier looking like a giant, half-crushed insect struggling to crawl out into the sea.

There were all types of people in Brighton too. It was a place full of both fortune and misfortune, a very tolerant, inclusive town. Because it was summer by then it would be teeming with visitors at the weekends too. I thought I could blend in there, go unnoticed for a while; maybe get my head clear, and find a job and another tenancy in order to put this time behind me. Or so I told myself.

Chapter 38

Wandering the streets, beachfront and narrow lanes of Brighton, jostling with crowds of happy tourists and purposeful shoppers, I felt like I had fallen off the edge of life and didn't know where or how to jump back on. It was soon high season and even the cheapest places were too expensive, especially at weekends. But I had no choice but to use my last credit card to pay for rooms in the cheapest B & Bs I could find. I couldn't see a choice. I had to put my head down somewhere at night, and had nowhere else to go.

One day the fortnightly money Brendan was sending didn't arrive on time. I went to a telephone booth down on the seafront to leave a message but, amazingly, this time his phone was on. He said the money would be there the following day, but that the next payment would be the last he could send. He wasn't going to be able to send anything after that. Something had gone wrong with all his plans. In a way I was relieved that he was finally admitting it, but I was exhausted, frightened and angry too – with him, but mostly with myself for having relied on him.

Standing in the phone box in Brighton, the sky darkening, and with absolutely no money left and nowhere to go, I wondered what would happen to me now.

Abandoned

'I'm sorry,' he whispered into the phone and I knew his wife or one of his family had come into the room, 'there's no more I can do.'

He put the receiver down and I was left listening to the dial tone and staring incredulously out at an angry, metallic-grey sea smashing against the black, ruined West Pier. I looked blankly along the promenade at all the people hurrying home through the drizzle but my legs wouldn't move. How had I allowed myself to get into such an impossible position?

Chapter 39

I stayed in the phone box going through the job ads in the local paper. I'd been phoning all week but most of them had already gone, or I didn't have the required experience. I rummaged in my bag for the section I'd ripped from a magazine months ago, and called the domestic employment agencies in the boxed ads again. Surely I could get some kind of live-in job. I had to.

'Remind us what kind of work you are after again,' one of the women asked. I tried to keep the desperation out of my voice but admitted I might consider anything. 'You're not really qualified and our clients are very particular, and anyway it's coming up to August. August is always a quiet month. Try again in September.'

'Okay,' I said, trying to keep my voice steady. 'Thank you, I will.'

'Hold one moment,' one woman at an agency I hadn't called before said.

I watched the coin meter ticking down on the phone and shook my bag, scraping about at the bottom for more coins. Sweat was pouring down my face and arms as she went off to check with her colleague about some recent details they'd had in. 'Yes, it's a governess position, for a

Russian family, working between Moscow and London. A boy of seven. Would you consider that?'

Would I consider it? I'd leap at it. I imagined all I'd get at that stage would be cleaner or carer jobs. I remembered how adorable boys of seven were, cheeky, curious and sweet. 'Yes,' I said, shoving the last coins into the slot, trying to sound casual, 'I'd definitely like some more details about it anyway.' She asked for my address to send details and an application form to, and I told her what I'd been telling all the others for months – that I was on holiday – and asked her to email them. She sounded suspicious but said she would.

'How soon do they want somebody?' I asked.

'As soon as possible, as far as I know.'

'Good.'

'Would that suit then?'

'Yes, it could do,' I said, trying to sound less desperate than I was.

'How soon could you start then?'

And then I messed it up, showing my desperation by saying, 'Straight away … I could be there by tomorrow really, if they needed me to.'

She said she'd email me details, but I never heard from her again.

I walked in a daze back to the B & B in Kemptown that I was booked into for another night. I couldn't believe Brendan was just stopping the money like that. I'd dreaded that from the beginning – of riding out all those delays, and then it all stopping abruptly when my own money had been used up and I was totally dependent. He'd always assured me that it wouldn't happen like that. But now it had, and I couldn't face dealing with it. I was too tired and shaky, ready to crack.

I stood aside for the owner as she passed me on the stairs with an armful of folded pink towels, smiling back at her as if nothing had happened. All my life that had been one of the most important things: not to let anyone know there was anything wrong or that I needed anything at all. I didn't know how to drop the charade now, even though I'd clearly needed help desperately for months.

I sprinkled drops of lemon essential oil onto my sponge and dropped it onto the shower tray, turning the shower to the hottest setting bearable. Sitting on the floor of the shower with my knees up and the scalding water pouring over me, I took long, deep breaths of the lemon steam to try to revive myself. Before seven o'clock, my skin red raw, I climbed under the covers. I lay staring up at the TV attached to a wall bracket in the corner of the room, without a thought or a plan in my head, as if nothing had happened. When my headache got worse I was frightened of turning off the sound and being forced to listen to my own thoughts. I rolled over and read Craig's coffee-ringed copy of *Jonathan Livingston Seagull*, which I'd discovered the day before, jammed down into the side pocket of one of the suitcases in the boot. I couldn't face thinking about what was going to happen next. There was no one to turn to. I knew I'd have no choice but to go to the authorities for help.

Eventually I lay there, trying to get to sleep, staring up at the wallpaper with its big, shiny, lilac flowers, worn and peeling in places. It was a single bed crammed between the wall and a large, old-fashioned wardrobe. I

Abandoned

don't remember much else about that bed or how I slept.
If I'd known that it would be the last bed I would sleep in
for nine months then I might have taken more notice.

Chapter 40

The first night of sleeping in the car was a mistake. I didn't plan it. I still had the last of the fortnightly money left, and Brendan had said he would be sending it one more time, plus I hadn't quite reached the limit on the last credit card. I probably had enough for a week or so in a B & B. But after I checked out of that last one I never went off to look for another. I was vaguely thinking of going back to London and throwing myself at the mercy of one of the employment agencies I'd been ringing, hoping that if they interviewed me in person they'd see how trustworthy and capable I was and find me some kind of live-in job. But by the evening I still hadn't plucked up the courage to leave Brighton.

I'd been sitting in the car unable to stop crying and wanted to wait until the puffiness in my face and eyes had gone down before I went off to find another B & B. I bought some chips from the stall on the pier, soaked them in vinegar, parked on the seafront and sat in the car to eat them, as I had done most nights, staring out at the sea.

I tried to think it all out, to see what the options were. I racked my brain for places I could go. But there was nowhere. I'd lost touch with everyone while I was with Craig. I felt too proud to get back in touch after more than two years and tell anyone how bad things had got for me. I'd wait until I was on my feet again.

I looked at the petrol gauge, wondering how much it would cost to drive to London, and whether I really should go back there the following day – even though there was no one for me left there. Mummy had gone to live in Spain several years before, so I couldn't go to see her. Even if she hadn't left, after my last visit to see her, I knew there was no way I'd visit again while my uncle was there. He had noticed I was even more nervous around him than usual last time. I knew that somehow he'd figured out I'd got myself into an abusive, 'controlling' relationship. I hadn't told anybody, but he laughed at me that day in a way that made my blood run cold and let me know that he knew. And I vowed never to go over to see them again until I'd got my life back together.

I kept hearing Craig's voice in my head saying: 'You'll come back to me. There'll be nowhere else for you to go …'

The beach was emptying, everyone around me preparing to go home. I pretended not to notice and didn't allow myself to imagine the warm, safe homes they might be hurrying off to. I blew on the chips one by one and tried to focus on what other options there might be before the money ran out completely. Where I could go? I seemed to have burnt all my bridges. I tried to imagine turning up at the various front doors of friends and colleagues I'd once known; tried to imagine myself explaining to them what had happened, what had become of my life, how little self-esteem I'd had to allow myself to be treated like that by Craig; what a spectacular failure I'd been. I knew I'd be too ashamed to tell anyone. I'd have to get through this my own way.

Abandoned

Sitting there, the tiredness of all those months suddenly caught up with me. I felt totally wiped out and heavy, as if a weight of wet sand had just been poured into my body, and I didn't feel able to drive off. I stayed sitting in the car after I'd finished my chips, staring out at the horizon, not wanting to walk into a B & B or hotel and be seen in that state. Night porters would have come on shift by then, watching out for anyone who booked into a single room but tried to sneak someone else up later. I'd been living like this for months now; I knew the suspicions, and couldn't bear another night of feeling like I was doing something wrong.

It was a warm evening but all that release of emotion had left me cold and shaky so I pulled a couple of fleeces out of my holdall and put one on. I rolled up the other fleece, put it down onto the passenger seat, leaned over and laid my head down on it; just to rest for a while and to think. I longed for a hot bath. I told myself I would get a room later in one of the cheaper hotels at the Hove end of town, which I hadn't been into before. In a small hotel I was more likely to get a room with a bath. It looked like I'd have to go to the authorities anyway so I might as well use the remaining credit on my card on that.

At close to 10.30 p.m. I locked the car doors, took the keys out of the ignition, loosened my boots, pulled up my legs and stretched myself out as much as I could across the front seats. It wasn't the most comfortable position, with the handbrake digging into my stomach, but it was only for a rest, so it was bearable. From that low down I could see nothing but a midnight-blue sky, which looked like glitter from a tube had been shaken across it. I couldn't see any people and it felt like no one could see in either, like I was almost invisible. I closed my eyes against a throbbing headache which had been rising up across the back of my head all evening, intending only to rest for half an hour or so. But I ended up falling into a deep, undisturbed sleep.

When I opened my eyes again there were clear blue skies and huge, screeching seagulls tilting slowly through it as a hot sun beat down through the windscreen. I was hot and sticky, my hair stuck to my forehead and the shirt under my fleece damp with sweat. For a moment I was disorientated, then shocked as I realised it was morning. I had spent a whole night in the car.

Chapter 41

After the first night it was easy to do it again; and then the next night and the next night after that. In a way it took some of the pressure off me. I had been running up all that credit card debt simply on accommodation night after night, to continue in a situation I didn't want to be in from the beginning. Suddenly I didn't have to spend anything at all. And for a couple of days at least there was an enormous sense of relief.

There was also a certain sense of freedom in knowing that I could survive without spending a penny on hotel bills or relying on anything or anyone. I no longer had to run around trying to find rooms for the night, always trying to conceal my state of exhaustion from receptionists, cleaners or night porters, or pretend I was just on holiday. After that first night, in a bizarre but quite misguided way, I felt I had got back some of the control over my life – although of course I was actually losing more control. But for a while I felt free, completely off the radar.

I had no idea I'd live like that in the car in Brighton for over a month in the end, seeing a shabbier and shabbier city every day. By eating chips and cheap, sugary foods I managed to live on the benefits money I was still getting.

There was no money for petrol any more, and definitely not for hotels. Very soon I realised I had swapped one trap for a worse one. But after a week of sleeping in the car I had no idea how to stop.

One of the worst parts of living in the car, especially during the August heat wave, was having nowhere to shower. You can only do so much washing in public toilets, even in the disabled ones where the hand basin and dryer are inside. Some days I changed into a bathing costume and waded out into the sea to wash as best as I could, but I never felt clean. All day I felt hot and grimy, the car smelling of sweat and the cheap takeaway food I ate in it. By the end of the first week the feeling of relief at not having to deal with people in hotels had gone and I dreaded every night.

Every part of me was stiff and aching, bruised or tender. I'd always been a heavy sleeper but in the car I woke up with the pain countless times during the night, rolling over or changing ends so that my head was at the other side of the car and my legs had a better chance of stretching out under the glove compartment. It would have been easier if I could have slept across the back seat, but it was piled high with all my possessions – boxes, bags, suitcases, everything that hadn't gone into storage.

After a few weeks my whole body physically resisted the night closing in, and I'd sit there fighting the tiredness as long as I could. Night after night I almost threw up at the thought of doing it again.

But without telling someone I didn't know how to stop it, and I was even more determined not to admit how I was now living to anyone. Because then I would have had to explain all the reasons why I was there, sleeping in my car – why I was alone in the world – and I couldn't bring myself to admit that, not even to myself.

I soon developed a routine. At first I parked up very late at night in the quieter squares around the hotels in central Brighton so I could run in to use their ladies' toilets to brush my teeth in the evenings, and wash more fully in the mornings before the traffic wardens arrived. Every morning I woke dripping in sweat with the sarongs and shirts I used to cover myself at night tangled around me.

I couldn't afford to waste petrol now that my money was running out, so I never drove too far during the day. I had a rota of hotels, so that nobody got too used to me anywhere. Usually I went to the big, swanky ones along the seafront: the Hilton or Metropol or Holiday Inn. It was more anonymous there, and although there were more doormen and concierges, there were also more people wandering in and out, crowds I could lose myself in. I still looked respectable enough to pass under everybody's radar then.

I knew the lobby layouts of most of the hotels by heart, so I could stride in confidently, as if I were a resident with a room key in my pocket, avoiding making eye contact with anybody and head straight for the ladies. Sometimes I took in a change of clothes or just clean underwear.

Once I'd washed and changed, filled up my water bottles and helped myself to some tissues, I walked out wearing what I came to think of as my 'car-pyjamas', with my boots and largest fleece on over the top. My car-pyjamas were just an old pair of baggy cords, several layers of long-sleeved tops and a long, brown, mohair-like cardigan, which until then I'd never worn, and which I threw over the sarongs covering me when the temperature dropped during the night.

If anyone saw me lying in the car, I imagined they'd think I might just have lost my door key or had too much to drink or been clubbing all night and slept in the car in my clothes until morning. Brighton is the kind of place where you could just about get away with that, at least for one night.

That is why I never slept in the same street twice – or the same position in the street anyway. The secret was to move around a lot so that nobody would ever get used to seeing me. The other secret was not to look too much like a female. I kept my neck and any bare skin covered and kept my socks on, sometimes wearing a spare pair over my hands. I thought that if someone just glanced in as they walked past and saw me lying there in a dark car, draped in all my dark layers, I wouldn't immediately look like a woman.

After I'd washed, and if I hadn't already changed into my 'nightclothes', I'd choose a street that I wasn't going to sleep in, one of the ones I would never sleep in. I'd park in the most discreet spot I could find – somewhere with tree cover, not too overlooked and not directly under lamp-posts. I'd sit there until as late as possible, waiting for it to get dark enough. Then I'd get ready for the night, covering myself with the sarongs as I hurriedly replaced each item of clothing I took off before removing the next one. I kept all my nightclothes and the sarongs and other things I used as blankets in one large yellow carrier bag on the floor, crammed into the area under the glove compartment during the day. I quickly learned it was easier to keep things separated and close to hand that way, so I didn't have to go fumbling about in different bags for things.

I'd then drive to the road I'd chosen to sleep in. I'd sit there for a while, making sure the coast was clear, sometimes having a snack from the 'food bag' I kept on the passenger seat floor. Once I'd lain down, I'd keep very quiet and will myself to sleep, covering my head with one of the sarongs if I heard anyone approaching. Soon I even convinced myself that because I couldn't see out, no one could see in either. It was that – the belief that I was almost invisible – which enabled me to do it night after night after night.

It was desperation for a shower that finally, almost a month later, got me to the day-shelter I'd noticed on one of the back streets. I hoped I'd get some food there as well. I'd already ventured to the door of the place a few times. The first time I couldn't even bring myself to go up the steps to enquire about what they did there, and the next two times it was closed.

This time it was open. I walked through the people sitting on the steps outside as if they were ghosts, trying not to see them or let any of them register me. A crackly voice at the other end of the intercom buzzed open the security door and I stepped inside.

It was dark inside and it took a while for my eyes to adjust, but when they did I saw it was a busy, well-run place. There was a strong smell of damp and stale sweat, but soon all I could smell was the delicious aroma of hot, meaty food. Everyone there must have been homeless but they were a diverse group and the atmosphere seemed relaxed and unthreatening; people standing around talking or sitting in groups or on their own eating from big plates of hot food. It had been ages since I'd eaten meat, or anything hot other than chips, and my mouth watered at the thought of it.

Everyone was busy and I felt awkward and out of place. After I'd spoken to one of the volunteers on duty – a small, thin girl with long, blonde dreadlocks decorated at the ends with silver and bronze beads – I had to wait for ages to get a towel and soap and permission to use the shower.

I stood in the corner hoping the light was dim enough to conceal my face as the girl with the dreadlocks hurried between tables, picking up plates and stopping to talk to some of the men. She was the first person I'd told about my sleeping in the car. I thought it would be a relief telling someone, but it was a shock hearing myself say it. Thinking it, and even doing it, was one thing, but actually hearing myself say it out loud to another person was another. I couldn't say 'she' is living in a car, as my brain wanted to say.

I had felt myself shaking as I spoke. I was short of breath and suddenly felt freezing cold. I didn't tell her much else about myself; when I started talking she seemed surprised by my accent, and suddenly became quite brusque. I felt she didn't think I was deserving of their resources, that there were 'proper' homeless people there in 'real' need, and that I was somehow wasting her time.

I stood there with my face burning in shame as I felt the stares of the men eating at tables nearby. I wanted the ground to open up and swallow me; and when I looked up and around me again at this unfamiliar, almost entirely male world I had stepped into I thought that maybe it already had.

Another woman on duty rushed up and handed me a towel and a small bar of pink soap. She showed me to a shower in the corridor next to a laundry room. The doors were tall but only three-quarter length so if someone climbed up they could look in over the top, but there was no one there when I went in and I was so desperate to have a shower that I didn't hesitate to use it. I crouched down to undress, hanging my clothes over the top. As I stepped under the hot water I started to cry, big, sudden sobs that took me by surprise. I let the water run down over my face and used the soap to scrub my face, body and hair vigorously.

Slowly I became conscious of loud voices in the corridor outside. It sounded like at least a dozen men were hanging around talking immediately behind the door. I checked the lock and held my breath. The voices became loud and aggressive. I picked up bits of talk about a fight some people had been involved in the night before at the marina.

'Do you know who's in there?' one of them asked loudly.

It suddenly felt like a club, like they all knew each other. For once I was glad to feel like an outsider.

'I dunno … Roy, is that you?' one of them called.

I was sure they knew I was in there. I heard titters, then silence, and wasn't sure whether to keep quiet or reply. I knew they couldn't see in unless they used a step or something, but I still felt vulnerable being naked in a shower with a door that didn't go up to the top and a large group of men standing outside. I bent down and tried to put a tough, streetwise tone in my voice, saying gruffly, 'No, I'm just finished though.'

Abandoned

I turned off the shower and quietly patted myself dry, hoping they'd leave, but they didn't. I stood there, perfectly still, wrapped in a towel, waiting, my hair dripping. When I realised they weren't going away I hurriedly put on the clean clothes I'd brought in with me. I stuffed the old ones down into my rucksack and left the shower, keeping my eyes down, just seeing a group of legs and torsos as they all stood aside with exaggerated gentlemanly gestures for me to pass. I mumbled my thanks but still had to brush up against one of them at the end of the narrow corridor when he didn't stand aside for me. I said, 'Excuse me' politely, trying to keep the nervousness out of my voice, and waited for him to move. I felt like he was waiting for me to look up at him, but I couldn't. I didn't want anyone to see my eyes, or to be forced to look into anyone else's. I didn't want to be pulled into their world; I didn't belong there – I couldn't hold my own. I wasn't strong enough, not yet anyway. I turned my face, trying not to let him see it.

'You're excused,' one of the others called down to him and he moved aside.

Another time I could maybe have smiled along, but the whole experience was humiliating, and I felt jumpy and on edge and didn't know whether they were tears or drips from my wet hair running down my face as I left. Apart from the workers, it seemed like I was the only woman in the whole place.

I was terrified I was on their radar, and that after that I'd be recognised by them all wherever I went in Brighton. By stepping into that day-shelter and showing my need I felt that I was somehow in their world – but I was still in denial about my own homelessness and couldn't bear even thinking about it. I felt intensely vulnerable and alone and vowed never to go there again. I didn't even stay for food. I walked away hungry, trying to ignore the hunger pains in my stomach just from the smell of it, looking back over my shoulder to check I wasn't being followed.

I didn't go straight to the car. I threaded in and out of the backstreets, returning to it the long way to be sure I wasn't followed. When I finally got to it and had the key in the lock I looked up and saw a man staring at me from across the way, standing hunched over in a doorway smoking. I was convinced he was one of the men from outside the shower, even though I didn't look up at them so didn't know what any of them looked like. I drove off in a panic, fear shaken loose inside me, thinking every man I passed was one of them, all of them knowing I was in Brighton on my own, sleeping rough in my car.

Chapter 42

I never went back to that day-shelter and tried to avoid that area of town completely but, over a fortnight later, exhausted and penniless, I finally drove to a night-shelter in a disused church in Hove. I realised I needed help, that I was stuck, not handling the situation; but getting help meant telling somebody and I didn't know who to tell, or how to put it into words. Telling a stranger, however, would be much easier than trying to go back to tell anyone in my past. After a lifetime of pretending that nothing was wrong, that I never had any problems, suddenly having to ask for help was almost impossible.

But things had got so bad that this time I was prepared to sleep there, at least for a night, just for a break from the car. I couldn't do it any more. I had been living in my car on the streets of Brighton for almost a month by then, and I'd been driving past the shelter for almost a week, trying to pluck up the courage to go in.

I spent a lot of time in churches during those weeks, sitting there, passing the hours, using them almost as safe-houses. One day I spoke to a priest who phoned the shelter for me and booked it. I arrived late, having spent hours outside in the car crying, wrestling with myself, telling myself that I shouldn't set foot in the place, that I didn't want them to recognise me the way I now imagined all the men who saw me in the day-shelter might.

I now wished I'd looked up at the men when I came out of the shower. The hardest thing was not knowing who they were. In the previous few days and weeks, when I'd been overtired, overwrought and slipping further and further off the radar, my mind played tricks on me and I looked at all men suspiciously, as if they were them. I started to fear them all indiscriminately – an almost hysterical, irrational fear.

The one time I'd been out to visit Mummy in Spain, my uncle had grown a long, scruffy beard. He was grey by then and even in the sun looked old and shabby and vague, like the men I now saw lurking in the doorways and shelters on the seafront. They all reminded me of him, and the knowing look he gave me the last time I saw him. That same look seemed to be in the eyes of all the men I soon hurried around Brighton trying to avoid, all saying 'This is what you get for telling.' I felt trapped in my own personal nightmare.

I was hungry and thirsty and couldn't bear another night in the car with my knees bent, jammed up against the steering wheel column all night, my neck forced into an almost broken position against the door, but I was still too frightened to go in.

I remembered doing advice work in Citizens Advice Bureaux and law centres, and working with the Mother Theresa Mission in Calcutta. I worked at Crisis at Christmas in London as well for a couple of years, partly because I didn't want to let my flatmates know I had nowhere to go myself at Christmas. I'd enjoyed the sense of camaraderie and community. I knew that most people who had ended up in that position had been hurt enough to have their hearts blown right open and would probably be the most compassionate, most understanding people.

But now everything felt different. What if I was wrong? What if I was putting myself in danger by being with them? Full of irrational fears, I felt too fragile and vulnerable, too alone and still too naive in many ways to take that risk.

I watched the night close in, the last of the light fading and the streets emptying. I was stiff and cold and dreaded lying down again. I tried not to lay my head directly on the car seat at night, knowing it was full of dust and crumbs and goodness knows what else, as my eyes got infected repeatedly: bloodshot and itchy from conjunctivitis. I worried they would get worse and affect my vision for driving. That would have been the end.

I still couldn't force myself to go inside the night shelter, though, and decided to sleep where I'd parked, partway down the steep street. I leaned over and lay across the seats, too shattered even to go through the most basic washing and changing clothes routine. I just pulled out the sarongs and the long brown cardigan from the yellow carrier bag on the floor and arranged them over me.

Within minutes I heard footsteps pass and then stop. I never heard them leave again and sensed someone was there. My heart raced. I tried to still my breathing in order to listen, terrified of raising my head to check. Finally I did, to find there was nobody there. I looked around at the silent unlit houses, and watched the wind through the trees fanning eerie shadows across the parked cars smeared with grey-gold street light. Until then I'd never really got that close to feeling fear about sleeping in the car. I was doing it on automatic pilot. I'd always parked up around the quiet terraces and crescents in mostly well-off areas once I found them, and didn't allow myself to think about the risks. This road felt too exposed and, despite my exhaustion, I was too nervous to sleep. I was about to drive off to a safer spot when I remembered the place booked for me at the night-shelter. At close to midnight I changed my mind. Tired and drained, my infected eyes dripping with pus, I decided to go in.

I buzzed the security door and spoke through the intercom to one of the night-workers. The CCTV camera swung round noisily to focus on me. I kept my voice low, wary of being overheard, and turned away from the camera, still trying to be invisible, even as locks clanked and the man I'd been whispering to through the intercom came to the main door to speak to me.

He said there was no record of a phone call made to them earlier about me, or anyone else.

'All the places are taken,' he said.

He let me in so he could check his logbook, even though he said he was almost 100 per cent sure. I followed close behind him to the main reception area. He poured me a coffee, and I looked around as he leafed through his notebook. It was all new blonde wood, brightly lit with a silver anglepoise lamp, clean and organised. It looked just like any other modern office area, not what I'd expected at all. It felt warm and safe and peaceful. Whatever happened, now that I had finally taken this step, I didn't want to leave: I couldn't bear the idea of going back out there. Inside, away from the dark and the traffic racing past, it was bright and quiet and smelt recently cleaned – nice cosy smells of furniture polish, hot coffee and what smelt like fresh-cut flowers. Maybe it was the tiredness, or the contrast after the previous few weeks, but I felt safe for the first time in months.

'Nope, definitely; nobody passed on any message,' he said, snapping his book closed before shuffling loose papers about on his desk. 'Anyway, it would be too late now. Last check-in is nine o'clock. Nobody can be checked in after that.'

'I just want a place until I get on my feet again.'

As I stood there, the plan I'd been fostering for weeks seemed possible again. I could live in a place like this, find a job and work during the day until I'd saved enough money to get a deposit and a month's advance to rent a room somewhere.

'Or just for the night,' I said, looking at his blank face. 'There's only a few hours left … Pleeeease,' I heard myself say.

He shook his head and said he couldn't; he wasn't allowed. I'd hit a wall of tiredness that had been catching up with me for months. I tried not to focus on the heaviness in my legs and wasn't sure if I was hallucinating when he pushed aside an empty plate smeared with yellow egg yolk, with a juicy grilled tomato at the edge. I swallowed hard and looked away.

I could feel tears running down my face and hear myself pleading. I felt humiliated doing it, especially when I saw the way his eyes lit up, almost as if he was enjoying my predicament. He leaned back on his chair and swivelled around to face me, his arms folded behind his head, looking me up and down as he told me the others were asleep now and that it would be wrong to disturb them by letting me in at this hour, even if he could.

Abandoned

'Anyway, they're mostly men, all sleeping on mattresses in the main body of the church. There are a few women in another part but they're long-term residents, recovering addicts who are here under a strict programme. We can't just let anyone in there with them for the night.'

I wanted to argue that I didn't do drugs or alcohol and wouldn't disturb them, that I'd never cause any trouble, that I wasn't just anyone. But of course I was – he didn't know me from Adam.

For weeks, as I'd driven past into Brighton, I'd seen men gathering by the front door in the evenings, milling about outside, waiting to be let in. I'd put my foot down as I drove off at the lights so that none of them registered me.

'Most of them are regulars,' he said, 'and men,' he repeated.

'You're being prejudiced,' I told him. 'You'd never treat your sister or your mother like this if they turned up here.'

'They'd never be in your position, not in a million years,' he replied, banging staples from his stapler against the edge of the desk.

Eventually he offered to let me sit in a chair in the small interview room, which was off at the side of the reception area where he would be all night. He offered to make me another coffee, saying I could get a few hours' sleep sitting there and he'd wake me in the morning before they changed shifts.

'It's the best I can do,' he said. I shook my head. I didn't want to sit up all night.

'Maybe I could find you a sleeping bag,' he said. 'We get deliveries of them to hand out, and I think there might be some left somewhere.'

Abandoned

I thought of the people I'd seen sleeping rough, huddled in sleeping bags in doorways first thing in the morning when I drove off to one of the hotels to wash. I didn't want to end up like that. I wouldn't … I told him how dangerous it was out there, that there must be something he could do for me, that I was utterly exhausted and just wanted to sleep.

'You can't just send me back out there; there must be something you can do, some responsibility you have towards people like me.' My own words shocked me: people like me? Who were these people like me?

He shook a cigarette from his pack and lit it, repeating his offer.

'I'm just a nightshift worker. I don't make the rules, I just follow them,' he said.

My legs were heavy and it felt like there were bits of glass under my eyelids when I blinked, but I refused the offer and said I'd prefer to go back out to the car. He shrugged, his hands flying out in an apologetic take-it-or-leave-it gesture, but he seemed to take offence, picking up his keys and getting up abruptly to let me out, saying, 'Suit yourself.'

Chapter 43

Two weeks after I'd tried to get into the night-shelter I was still in Brighton, still sleeping in my car, still trying to be invisible and not to fall any further. But I felt myself spiralling out of control. My life was just about survival then, and I couldn't think beyond it. I felt trapped – detached and disorientated and exhausted but still trying to pretend I wasn't. I'd been two days without food, and had no idea where to turn.

The name of the vicar who ran the night-shelter flashed into my head and I vaguely remembered that his telephone number was up in small letters on the board outside. I went up to check, and when I called him he said to come up and have a chat

It's awful to go to churches just for the tea and the hope of a plate of biscuits but that was on my mind as much as anything as I walked up the hill past all the big Victorian houses.

While he went off to make a pot of tea I sat in his big, airy front room looking out at the street, almost shocked at the quietness. I tried not to look at the settee or focus on how much I wanted to lie flat out on it. Photographs in silver frames of smiling blonde children and teenagers were on show on the lid of a shiny black piano and across the white walls. I found myself wishing it was me, not them, who lived in this calm, safe, happy atmosphere, with someone like him to cherish me.

Half a dozen light-blue leather suitcases and holdalls were standing in the doorway to the hall.

'We're off on holiday for two weeks in the morning,' he explained, coming back in. 'So there's probably not a whole lot I can do for you at this stage. But tell me briefly what it is.'

He set a tray of tea things noisily onto the table. I stared at the packet of chocolate biscuits. 'It's okay,' I said, 'it doesn't matter. I just wanted a chat really.'

I didn't know what else to say. There seemed no point telling him what had happened, that I'd ended up living in my car. There was nothing he could do if he was going on holiday. I didn't know what else I was prepared to risk saying.

'I just don't know if I believe in God any more,' I heard myself say, snapping a biscuit in half.

For a moment he stopped stirring his tea, narrowed his eyes and looked me straight in the eye, as if I was wasting his time completely. But then he poured the tea, shook biscuits from the packet and chatted amiably about faith and what God meant to him. A white kitten rubbed itself against my leg and all I really wanted to say was that if I lived in a big, warm, cosy house like this, I would probably believe in God again too.

I hated the bitterness creeping into my thoughts, hated the person I was becoming. I don't know how long I sat there with my head hanging down, but he reached across the table and pressed an almost weightless hand over mine.

'Whatever you might think of Him, God will never stop believing in you. Never forget that.'

I was stunned at the warmth and softness of his hand over mine, and how protected it made me feel. I never wanted him to remove it, but I knew any second he would, so I nudged it away and rattled my cup back onto the saucer. I saw him looking anxiously at his watch and made a move to go, but then I glanced out through the large bay window on to the cold grey street. I knew there was no one else I could go to and that I wouldn't be able to come back here to talk to him for at least another two weeks. I couldn't survive another two weeks of this. My heart started thumping and I quickly blurted out that I'd just remembered there was something else I was going to ask him.

'What's that?'

I told him about living in the car, trying not to make it sound as bad as it was, and asked for his advice. Could he see anything I wasn't seeing, any solution to it?

'No wonder you're so stressed,' he said, advising me to go back to the shelter and talk to the case-workers there.

The word 'case-worker' sent shivers through me, making me think of the legal advice I used to give people. I didn't need a case-worker! I just needed a way back in and a rest, so that I could do it for myself. He asked if he could phone them for me and see if they could book me in for a chat later that afternoon.

'Just go to talk to them,' he said. 'There must be something they can do. They'll ring around, see what's available, especially for someone who they can see just needs a hand back into life.'

Before I left he made me promise I'd do it. Because he was so nice and had gone to the trouble of phoning the centre, I felt I should at least go in for a chat. Maybe I'd get another cup of tea too.

I walked straight past it down to the seafront, killing a few hours watching the crowds. The sun was out again and I sat on a bench and watched children splashing about in the sparkling water, the younger ones running in and out of the tide, squealing in delight at the shock of cold sea water on their bare skins.

By the time I'd summoned the courage to go back there to at least talk to them it was already after five and all the case-workers had left for the day. The guy who had taken the phone call from the vicar – a thin young Asian man in tight black jeans ripped at the knees and a long purple jumper – was called to come and have a chat with me. He dragged another chair into the small side room, propped the door open, and asked what he could do for me. I didn't know where or how to start, or even how much I was prepared to tell him. He looked too young to confide in.

'What *can* you do for people?' I asked. He told me some of the things they could do, cases they had dealt with. He was softly spoken, very calm and a good listener. I felt myself regaining some of my stillness sitting opposite him and ended up telling him about my relationship with Craig, the money I'd been waiting to get back from Neil, the promise from Brendan, and how I'd started sleeping in my car and now didn't know how to stop. He was wearing leather flip-flops under his jeans and sat there, big-eyed and nodding, as I spoke, playing with an elastic band wrapped around his fingers.

Apart from the vicar, the blonde woman in the day-shelter and the last few phone calls to Brendan when I told him not to phone again, I hadn't spoken more than a few words to anyone for months. My voice was thin and scratchy, but this time it was a relief to talk and things came spilling out. After almost two hours of talking I felt drained and hollowed out inside. I was cold and trembling with emotion, and suddenly aware of my hunger and how long it was since I'd eaten.

He asked if I was hungry and I stared at the radiator and nodded, embarrassed to admit it. It was Friday and he told me sacks of Marks and Spencer's food, just past its sell-by dates, had arrived. He took me out into the reception area to go through them, telling me to take whatever I wanted. I wouldn't be able to talk to anyone until Monday, so he suggested I came back then.

'Take enough for the next few days,' he said.

I pulled out a poached salmon sandwich and told him that was enough, suddenly feeling too sick to eat anything. He gave me a bowl of pasta salad, a Thai noodle salad and a bag of doughnuts and told me to keep them for the weekend. While he went to check something I tore open the wrapping and ate a sugary doughnut almost without pausing for breath, washing it down with another mug of tea that the girl on reception brought in. I could feel the life seeping back into me.

Slumped back in the chair I felt all floppy and warm and didn't want to move. I realised I'd let my guard down a bit too far and felt raw and unprotected. It was intensely uncomfortable having people see me this vulnerable, knowing I had no family to go to. I'd pretended all my life that I had this close, loving family looking out for me, and letting the illusion go wasn't easy; it was bringing my whole emotional scaffolding clattering down around me. Before the guy came back with the appointments book I got up and walked down the corridor towards the exit. When the door buzzed for someone to come in I slipped out, back on to the street, and walked quickly up the hill towards the car.

I drove off eating the sugary doughnuts, convinced that if I'd stayed to get help from him I would have been stuck in Brighton, lost in the system there forever. I didn't feel strong enough yet to do it all for myself again, but I didn't trust the system to help me put myself back together either. I needed more time to think. Being in the car one more night wouldn't kill me.

Chapter 44

I realised I had to stop drifting, that no one was going to look after me or do it for me. I was not a child any more, no matter how vulnerable I felt. I had to get my act together: get a job, find another home and start again. I had to forget the money from Brendan, and the dream of being part of a proper family with him. I was never going to get that now.

The following day, on the pavement outside the Odeon on the seafront, I saw a man half-lying on the ground with a crowd gathered around him. An ambulance flashed and wailed its way through the traffic towards them and I wandered over behind the others. He was obviously a vagrant – shabby and vulnerable, on his own like me – and had a cut on the side of his head dribbling black blood. I vaguely recognised him; thought that I'd sat in the same café as him when my benefit money had come through a few mornings before, and I'd gone in for an all-day breakfast. There was an open can of Special Brew in his jacket pocket and a thick paperback in the other. When I looked at him again I saw he was staring through the crowd directly at me like I was his salvation. I felt I should do something, smile even, but feared I was being pulled into another world, swallowed up into something I didn't want to be part of. I couldn't bear even being recognised by him. I turned and almost ran.

I was still in denial that I was homeless like all the other homeless people I came into contact with, but I could see how fast I was sliding towards where he had ended up. I knew I had to get out of Brighton. It was too small; I was being recognised, and soon there would be no going back. Returning to London was the best option. It was the only place I'd ever felt at home. All the other places I'd stopped in temporarily when driving aimlessly around the country hoping to find a place I could put down roots had just felt more and more alienating.

I'd only left London because of Craig. I'd just fled, frightened to be there any more, frightened of him catching up with me again, of his madness creeping in under my skin. But now I was beginning to see that I was running as much from all the emotional stuff that our relationship had opened up in me, as I was from him. I could see I'd been wrong to let him drive me out. London was where the jobs and the opportunities were. London was something I needed to face again. I was not going to let him control my life with fear as my uncle once had. Unless I fought back now I knew I'd be trapped in a cycle of abuse forever. My decision to leave made me feel as if I was taking charge of my life again.

Chapter 45

The day I drove away from Brighton was warm and sunny. For the first time in months I felt clear and strong and full of hope. It felt like Craig couldn't hurt or control me any more; it felt like I'd moved on, that I'd got things into perspective again.

I knew I'd have to face some nights sleeping in the car when I got to London, but it wouldn't be for long: I was ready to ask for help now to get back on my feet. I'd go to the housing agency straight away and call the homeless charity, Crisis, and some of the other homeless organisations to see what help was available. So I hoped it would only be for a few more nights ... a week or so at most. The end was definitely in sight.

And once I got there I'd find a job too. Even if it was just sweeping floors, it would give me a way to get some money together for a deposit on a flat. I'd throw myself back into life. I wasn't going to let this beat me.

I stopped off at a convent on the way, to return a book I'd borrowed and to talk through my plans with one of the nuns. I'd stayed in their guesthouse for a few nights, a few weeks before that first night in the car, and had found the nuns there to be strong, compassionate, surprisingly worldly women, who were very easy to talk to.

Abandoned

I sat in front of the blue enamelled crucifix that hung over the altar in their little wood-clad chapel, thinking out my plan and praying that I'd have the strength to cope with whatever happened once I got back to London. I left feeling strong and together, and certain that going back was the right thing to do.

One of the nuns very generously gave me £20 to help with the petrol for the drive back but I used it for supplies instead, thinking it was Friday and that my benefit money would be in my account that morning to pay for petrol. But I had lost track of the days again: it was only Thursday. As I drove away I panicked, realising I might not have enough fuel for the journey. As I entered London the gauge showed almost empty.

There was no credit left on any of my credit cards by then and I had only about £4 in cash left and no cheque guarantee card. I considered parking up somewhere and waiting for my benefit money the following morning but knew I'd probably just be towed away. In the end I decided to stop at the next garage and use one of the cheques I still had left to pay for fuel.

The next garage I came to was a small, privately owned business with just two pumps outside. I was concerned about looking the cashier in the eye, knowing I hadn't got the money in my account right then to pay for it. But cheques take at least two days to clear and by then my benefit money would definitely be there to cover it, so I managed to talk myself into doing it. I knew if I went in and asked if I could use a cheque without a guarantee card they would definitely say no. I didn't know what else to do. I said a prayer and filled up.

Abandoned

I gave the cheque to the cashier, making a play of not being able to find my cheque card. He said he had been told not to accept any cheques without a card and phoned the manager. She and her husband came in and I tried to convince them that there was money in my account. But the woman insisted on phoning my bank and they told her that they wouldn't honour it.

She wouldn't believe there was no other way for me to pay, or no one for me to call to pay for me.

'There must be a relative or friend you can call,' she said.

But there wasn't. I had let my life unravel so much while I was with Craig that there was no one left at all. In the end she got really angry and threatened to call the police, but I still couldn't find a solution. I tried to stay calm and promised to drive back the following day to pay them in cash but she refused that. She would only let me go, she said, if I left behind my tax disc and came back later for it. I couldn't do that; so she locked the door and called the police. I knew I was in the wrong but the petrol was already in the car and the cheque would definitely have cleared when the money went into my account the following day. I tried to reason with her but I was shaking, and by the time the police arrived I was having a full-scale panic attack.

We went out to the car. When the police took down some details and asked me for my address I refused to tell them. They were understandably suspicious and got quite angry, telling me they could arrest me. In the end I gave them my old Newcastle address, which was where the car was still registered. They still seemed really suspicious though. When I said there was no one in London I could call to pay over the phone with a credit card for me, they asked me how I intended to drive all the way back up the motorway to Newcastle if I had no money and only one tank of petrol. I had no answer. The woman from the garage was shouting that I was a criminal and a liar trying to steal their hard-earned profits; her husband was telling her to calm down but agreeing with her, threatening to siphon out the petrol with some rubber tubing, which he'd dragged over from the repair shop. I just wanted to run from the forecourt screaming that I didn't have an address, that I was homeless! Fortunately, no words came out and on the outside I stayed calm.

I shut down standing opposite the five of them as one of the policemen radioed through to get more details about the car, and the manageress continued to call me a thief and a criminal. I'd never done anything criminal in my life and yet here I was being accused and shouted at by the manager and her husband. I was shaking inside and could hardly hold myself upright, but I knew that all she could see was my stony face as I stared straight ahead trying to imagine myself back into the calm of the silent chapel I'd sat in that morning. But I couldn't, any peace I'd had that morning had completely gone.

The police agreed to let me go, but warned that if the cheque didn't clear I'd be arrested. I knew that it would clear, but I was visibly shaken. I was shocked at their aggression and hostility towards me and felt so totally alone.

Here I was in London, the city where I was born and had spent most of my life, and there was nowhere to go and no one to go to. I wasn't prepared for how isolated I would feel. *Was Craig right? Would I be driven back to him after all?* He was the only person I knew left here really. One telephone call to him and I wouldn't have to spend another night in the car, or stand in front of more strangers somewhere being shouted at and feeling so low. It would be utter madness, of course, and I absolutely wouldn't do it.

For the first couple of nights in London I parked in a quiet, one-way street where Nighthawk security guards came out of one of the driveways and walked up and down past the car, staring in at me but saying nothing. I wasn't entirely sure at that stage whether sleeping in your car was illegal or not, but I assumed it wasn't. They didn't question me or move me on, and I was so exhausted that eventually I managed to shut them out enough to fall into a restless, broken sleep.

Sleeping in the car in the residential streets of London was harder than it had been in Brighton, where I had convinced myself that sleeping in a car was almost acceptable, given the clubbing scene down there – I could just have been clubbing and too drunk to drive home. But here there were neighbourhood watches, twitching curtains, traffic wardens and private security men patrolling the posher streets.

In the depression I was in, all I wanted to do was sleep all day but I woke up early to dress and get the car and myself looking respectable. I brushed my teeth with bottled water and washed my face with wads of toilet paper soaked in water before driving off to find a McDonald's or a hotel bathroom to wash properly in, well before the traffic wardens started for the day.

Abandoned

After the first couple of nights I parked on different roads every night. A lot of my time and petrol was taken up just trying to find 'safe' ones. The incident at the garage had completely destroyed any confidence I'd had about coming back to London, and I felt more and more fearful about everything. I was feeling as low as I had when I left London in the first place. All my defences were up again; it was just me against the world.

Some mornings, as I sat in the car eating breakfast, commuters would see me as they made their way to work. I dreaded the looks most of them gave me, but some of them seemed almost scared of me: glancing in nervously and then looking away, all of us trying to out-scare one another. I knew none of them would confront me. Anyway, I'd done nothing wrong. I told myself that I wouldn't see them again so it didn't matter, but I felt increasingly ashamed of myself for how I was living and for not knowing how to stop.

Soon I began to notice the same milkmen rattling down streets early in their floats, the postmen pulling their red carts around, the workmen eating breakfasts in their vans, reading papers with their feet up on the dashboards until it was time to start. It wasn't long before I began to feel recognised and watched by them all. I was mostly sleeping in the same few 'safe' streets I'd found. I felt trapped in the area, subsisting on the benefit money, which wasn't enough to allow me to drive far out of London again or do much else. More and more of my energy went into trying to conceal my situation and just survive, rather than finding a way out of it.

I did go to the housing advice centre a few days after arriving back in London but they wouldn't even give me the most basic information without me telling them my address. But I didn't want to tell them who I was at that stage or that I was homeless. I thought that my benefit money would stop if I did. It was the same when I phoned some of the homeless charities – Housing Justice, CHAS and Shelter. All I really wanted was help with getting together a month's deposit and a month's advance but none of them seemed able to give that. It seemed an obvious solution to me but I suppose they thought I'd spend it on drink or drugs.

All the organisations I phoned wanted more information before they would tell me what other help they might be able to provide. After the incident with the police taking down my details, and not being one hundred per cent sure if it was legal to sleep in a car anyway, I was wary, and reluctant to give them any details. Especially since I knew they were probably only going to advise me to go in person to the local Homeless Person's Unit. I was too afraid of losing my benefit money to do that, even though it wasn't housing benefit I was getting. I also knew I wasn't a 'priority homeless' person, so short of just registering me I knew they couldn't do much else.

For the next few weeks, as everything spiralled out of control again, I spent my days mostly in the car dodging the traffic wardens or feeding parking meters with money intended for food. I tried to think things through, but the worse the situation got the more difficult it was for my mind to focus on my problems. Mostly I'd spend the time just sitting, my head completely blank, or working out which street I was going to park in that night, or reading until I spotted a traffic warden and had to drive off again, all the time watching the petrol gauge. It felt like they were making a game of it, spotting my car and then getting on their radios and telling the others. Every corner seemed to hide another one. I felt as if my car was being shunted around a giant board as I drove off around the corner until another one appeared.

I was applying for jobs online in the library every day, still convinced I could get a job and work, sleeping in the car until I earned the money I needed to rent somewhere. But more and more of my effort was going into just surviving – finding somewhere to park each night and eking out the money so there was enough for petrol and food – and just concealing my situation from the world.

I was washing in pubs and hotel toilets but I couldn't find anywhere for a shower or to wash my hair; and in the end that was the thing that almost had me going to the homeless shelters in London, just as it had in Brighton. I couldn't smell myself any more but knew it couldn't be nice.

I was living in one of the most expensive cities in the world on virtually no money but still trying to eat well to keep my strength up and prevent my mind from flipping completely: fruit and raw veg, nuts and yoghurt and tinned sardines. But hot food was what I craved and I could only afford chips, Macdonald's or cartons of egg-fried rice. Because I had to buy petrol and live on takeaway food I never had enough to make ends meet. The last few days at the end of every fortnight, before my next benefit money arrived, I would have little, if anything, to eat.

About a month after arriving back in London, when the cold weather finally set in, I bought a sleeping bag – searching the Argos catalogue for the cheapest I could find. For three whole days that week I ate nothing but

Abandoned

some sour apples I picked from a tree in the walled garden of an empty house. I'd noticed the side gate unlocked when I'd walked past before and was tormented by the apples I could see fallen under the tree. I was at my wits' end the next time I walked past, weak, light-headed and almost hallucinating with hunger. I took a deep breath and went in, locking the gate to the street behind me, and sat on the wet grass under the tree eating them and crying. It was a new low. I felt so alone and just didn't know what to do. I went back several times in the next couple of days, sitting there on the damp grass in the blissful silence. Those apples were the nearest to theft that I came.

I eventually found some food stalls in Camden market where at closing time the hot Chinese food was sold off at one pound instead of almost five pounds. It was a revelation. Other homeless-looking people like me seemed to emerge from the shadows at the same time and slip in through the after-work crowd, and I felt the people behind the stalls picking us out from the crowd, putting up one finger to let us know that it was only one pound, while they continued to charge the work crowd full price. I felt like I had 'homeless' tattooed on my forehead. I felt humiliated and degraded, but not enough to turn away.

Chapter 46

Sometimes my phone, which I was using as an alarm clock, would run out of charge and I'd oversleep. I'd end up getting parking tickets I had no way of paying, just as I had in Brighton when I ran into shops to buy food, or, getting lost in the unfamiliar streets, returned to the car after the ticket from the meter had expired. One day, a Portuguese traffic warden who I was always trying to avoid – after he'd seen me waking up in the car late one morning – must have taken pity on me. He had already given me a few tickets. Putting another one under my wipers as I ran back late, he told me about a hospital car park not too far away which was off-limits to them.

'Do you ever park there?' he said. I shook my head and unlocked the car, too tired to even be embarrassed in case he smelt the inside of it. 'Hospital security staff check the cars themselves there,' he said, 'but I don't think they're as thorough as we are.' He winked conspiratorially.

That same afternoon I headed there and it was true; there was a sign saying it was a private car park. And there were no traffic wardens. At last I could leave my car somewhere and not feel hounded by them. It was an enormous relief and instantly took some of the pressure off me. For the first week I paid in the machines and could afford to stay long enough to wash in the hospital toilets and have a cup of tea and maybe some food in the canteen in the mornings. Then one day I came back late and found that no one had given me a ticket.

A few days later again I had run out of money but I desperately needed a wash so I risked it. I crossed my fingers in my pocket, hung my blue-glass Rosary beads from the rear-view mirror and left the car park without paying. Although it was wrong I did it day after day after that, and never once got a ticket. I noticed that a lot of the other cars had notices up on the windscreens saying 'obstetrician …' or 'surgeon …' or 'midwife …' '… on call', together with a bleep number on which to contact them. So most days I put one up too, inventing a bleep extension and praying that the security guards wouldn't check and try to contact me on it.

I had only been in London for a few weeks but it already felt like months, and I was going almost insane just from not being able to take a shower anywhere. For all those months, ever since I was last in London with Craig, I wasn't having periods, which almost felt like a blessing now when I was sleeping in a car without anywhere to shower. It would have been a worse hell if I had been menstruating every month. After lots of tests the consultant I'd seen in Newcastle couldn't find any other reason for it than stress. I didn't know that that could happen just through stress.

'Oh, you can die from stress,' she said, telling me that once I got my life back on an even keel things would right themselves.

Since then I'd been driving around the country living in different places every week or couple of nights for almost a year, and had now ended up living in the car. I didn't know how much more stress my body could take. No wonder it had shut down.

There were a couple of large hotels near the hospital and I was also using their facilities to wash in, or I would wait for pubs to open to use theirs, visiting them on a rota basis as I did with the hotels in Brighton so that nobody became too familiar with me. But you can only do so much washing in public toilets. I felt incredibly grimy and degraded, constantly aware of a sour, unclean smell from my hair and clothes. I was at an all-time low. Rushing back and forth looking a mess each morning, threading in and out among the commuters with my tatty carrier bag of wash things, I felt increasingly ashamed of myself and ground down. Then one day in the hospital I found a shower. And it felt like a miracle.

It was just an untiled, concrete space at the back of the toilets, with a vented window that let in the cold. I discovered it by accident, turning into a corridor I'd never been down before to avoid a security guard who was coming towards me. The water was scalding at first after the cold outside, but once I'd braved the cold to get undressed and stood under it, I never wanted to get out. I stayed for hours the first time, scrubbing myself from head to foot and thawing out completely, feeling my muscles trying to lengthen, especially in my neck, which was cramped up against the car door night after night.

There was a lockable door at the back of the toilets, blocking the shower area off, and I got used to being the only one ever in there using it. The first time someone rattled the door and knocked, calling out that she wanted to use it, I panicked, remembering the men outside the shower in the day-shelter in Brighton. There weren't any curtains or dividing walls, but there were two shower heads, so two people could use it at the same time. I didn't want to share, embarrassed to be seen changing back into my shabby clothes and dirty boots. I unlocked the door and rushed back under the steaming water while a woman undressed, staying in the corner where she couldn't see me from the changing area.

She was an Australian woman, tall and blonde. She chatted away, through the wall to the changing area, as if she knew me, like I was a normal human being. I tried to think what to say back, to remember what girls talked about, small talk. I'd kept myself to myself all these months, and apart from the odd reply here or there it had been ages since I'd spoken to anyone. But all I could think of was my pile of shabby clothes on the bench outside and my boots hanging from the vented window to air.

She didn't seem to notice though. She stepped in with her blonde hair pinned up and just a small pink hand towel, leaning across me to hang it up. I was embarrassed at my dry, pale skin next to her smooth tan, and my swollen feet with their yellowed, overgrown nails. Hobo feet.

She told me she lived nearby and cycled into work late, and asked me if I did too. She had no idea I was homeless; she thought I worked there. I couldn't believe I could still get away with that. She had a kind, open face and her voice was so warm and relaxed I was afraid I might tell her the truth about where I was living. I bit down on my lip and faced the wall, forcing myself not to weaken, not to blurt out the truth to her, concentrating instead on the steam of her apple shampoo, which made me hungry again.

Abandoned

I didn't have a towel, so tried to put a laugh into my voice as I stepped out and shouted that I'd left it 'at home' as I patted myself dry with loo roll.

'I'm always doing that,' she said, offering me hers. I felt like I'd made a new friend, but then reminded myself that I wasn't in a position to make friends with anyone. We were in different worlds now.

'It's okay,' I replied, hurrying to leave, 'I'll manage.'

Finding cheap places to eat in London is not easy. But as long as I was only buying snacks instead of full meals I was able to eat in the hospital canteen fairly cheaply. I would get back in touch with the housing charities sporadically when I felt able. But I felt like I was in a dark tunnel – all I could think of was getting an advance and month's deposit for privately rented accommodation. The worse I got the more terrified I was of going to live in a hostel, which, since I clearly didn't fall into any 'priority homeless' category – being a single, childless woman without disability – was the best I could have hoped for.

A few of the charities said they would make enquiries about the possibility of getting the deposit and month's rent in advance, and would get back in touch with me when they had some news. However, my mobile phone was hardly ever on as I could rarely afford to put credit on it, only using it as an alarm clock, and they never left messages. I knew how busy they all must have been and that I should have been more persistent with them, but I realised I had to get my mind strong before I could do that. Otherwise I thought I'd be carted off to a mental hospital rather than be helped to find somewhere to live and a job. I lost track of days, and again the weeks were slipping into months.

I had managed to stay relatively anonymous in the hospital for several weeks. But there was a community in there and I soon started to recognise some of the hospital 'characters': the locals who just seemed to sit around in there; the patients down in their dressing gowns to have a smoke, some wheeling themselves around the quieter corridors in new wheelchairs. And I soon started to worry that people were recognising me.

Almost every day, in the corridor between the entrance to A & E and the lifts, I'd see a man in a green towelling dressing gown, a silk, paisley cravat bunched at the neck, who looked like a dark-haired Kenneth Williams. He would follow the blue line along the corridor right down to the lifts, slow-dancing with his drip, humming loudly as he two-stepped along, smiling at all the staff rushing past. Nobody seemed to be smiling back at him though. Soon I began to think I was hallucinating, and that they weren't smiling at him because they couldn't see him – that my worst fear had come true and I had already lost my mind.

Fortunately, I found lots of out-of-the-way places in the hospital to sit. Whenever I felt that I was becoming too familiar down in the canteen, I would wander around finding a place to sit or read. Sometimes I would join the queues sitting around outside the clinics, hoping I blended in and that people would excuse the way I looked because they would assume I was ill. It felt fantastic to be off the streets, to be able to shower in the basement and eat in the canteen, and to sit around not being judged too much, all the time knowing that my car was safe in the car park. I spent more and more time there. The hospital was like a big city inside, and it soon became my world.

One day in the canteen I realised I'd left my purse in the car once I'd reached the till with my food. I didn't usually eat hot food down there; even though it was cheaper than any place outside it was still too expensive. But that day I had. I knew I had money in my purse to pay for it so instead of the food going cold I asked if I could eat first and 'go home' to get it afterwards.

The tiny Filipino manageress said she wasn't allowed to do that, but insisted on lending me the money from her own pocket. The way she looked at me let me know she understood how difficult things were for me. I was surprised by her kindness and grateful, but still found it almost impossible to accept – I hated anyone knowing.

She said I could pay her back the next day. I told her again that the money was 'at home' and I'd get it as soon as I'd eaten. I said 'at home' too loudly, hoping the other people in the queue overheard me, enjoying them thinking I had a home somewhere to go back to. We both blushed and avoided one another's eyes when I said it, and suddenly I felt sure she knew it was a lie. Maybe she'd seen my car in the car park, loaded up to the roof with all my stuff, or seen me go in and out of the showers every morning, or just noticed I was wearing more or less the same clothes in there every day.

As soon as I'd eaten I went to get my purse to repay her. But I knew I hadn't fooled her. Whenever I went in there afterwards I'd be too uncomfortable to stay if she was on duty. I'd feel her eyes on me the whole way across the canteen, my back burning with shame as I walked straight through and burst through the double doors at the end to go in search of another part of the hospital to sit in.

But the canteen was the only place I could get a free cup of tea, so I never went very far from it. There were big urns of boiling water at the back and I'd bring in my own tea bags in my pocket. If any of the staff did see me they must have turned a blind eye.

The staff must have suspected there was something odd about me, sitting there on my own day after day, evening after evening. But they were kind and never rushed me out. Pretty soon they must have realised I wasn't a patient or a visitor, and even though most of them gave me staff discount, they must have known I didn't work there either. They didn't say anything, though, or ask me to show a card; they just rang up the discounted prices while I stood there, trying to think myself out of my body in order to keep my dignity.

One evening there was a new girl on the till who asked if I was staff. I was about to say, 'No, visitor,' but the other manager, a middle-aged Mediterranean-looking man, came past and said quietly, 'Yes, she's staff,' and then just walked off, giving me a small nod. I had to fight back the tears, realising that my circumstances, which until then I had thought I was concealing from most people down there, were probably an open secret. I don't think they realised I was living in my car, just that I was going through a bad time. And even though I found it hard to accept at the time, their kindness meant a huge amount to me.

There was a chapel in the hospital too. When I wasn't in the canteen or upstairs in the library I would often be

Abandoned

there, mostly because it was quiet and warm. I half-expected other homeless people to be there too. But the security guards made regular checks and occasionally I saw them ask people to leave. Fortunately, I still looked respectable enough to pass as a patient or visitor. It was always open so whenever I needed a sanctuary from the people, cold, ugliness or hostility I was facing outside I would end up there, sitting on one of the hard wooden chairs at the back. I would read for hours in there, or do crosswords to keep my brain alive; or just sit there thinking or praying. Sometimes, if there was no one else about, I would drag a chair behind the stained-glass altar screen and try to sleep.

I don't know where else in London I would have found a place to shower every day, and a place where I wasn't getting parking tickets, and because of that I very soon felt trapped in this small corner of London. I'd had another piece of luck too. I didn't have to drive around locating 'safe' streets to sleep in any more. About a month after I arrived I discovered a laneway at the edge of some woods, and for the next seven months or so it became my home.

The laneway was long and narrow, crowded on both sides with tall trees coiled in ivy. It was full of the damp smell of the woods and during the day clear green light, which filtered down through overhanging branches. From where I parked, under bushes against one of the high banks, I could see nothing but trees. Sometimes I heard traffic from the road at the top but it sounded more like the sea and being there always felt like being a million miles from anywhere. It took me a while to get used to the silence and the dark, but I didn't mind the isolation. It was a relief after being stared in at first thing in the morning in residential streets.

I didn't allow myself to think of the dangers – I had detached from almost everything by then. The depression numbed a lot of the fear. Most of the time during those months I couldn't think or concentrate, I was barely functioning. I'd spend hours just staring out at the trees in 'my' laneway, as I soon came to think of it, watching the evening and morning light, the birdlife and animals, getting back there earlier and earlier, grateful to be away from the bustle and aggression of the city streets.

For the first few weeks I never saw any other cars there at night, and soon the laneway began to feel like home. It was a huge relief to have a place to come back to every evening – to no longer have to drive about looking for different streets to sleep in. I could just about afford the petrol to drive between there and the hospital car park each day and when I had done all I had to during the day I drove back to it almost eagerly. When I got there, if I hadn't eaten it already, I'd divide the baguette, which was my usual evening meal, into three, open a tin of sardines and make two sandwiches. I'd save the third piece for breakfast. After eating I'd just sit there staring out at the dark or lie in my sleeping bag across the front seats, waiting for sleep to come.

Towards the end of the first month there things changed. I was just falling asleep when the headlights of another car suddenly swung into the laneway. It parked up a few car lengths from mine, the engine still idling. Drum and Base music thudded over the sound of the engine and I heard loud voices, laughter and the sound of doors slamming. Footsteps crunched in the undergrowth in the woods. Strong winds snapped across the sky and fallen branches and dry leaves rolled noisily about the laneway. Suddenly I realised how very alone and vulnerable I was out there. No one would hear my screams.

I rubbed cautiously at a small area of the windscreen with my elbow. A collage of wet leaves was already stuck to the outside. It was impossible to see who was there, or what they might be doing. Fighting waves of panic, I reached for my mobile, but suddenly realised there was no one to call. I quickly pressed it for the time: it was 11.22 p.m. My car was pointing in the right direction to drive straight off, as I'd always planned to do if another car pulled up. But my whole body had frozen with fear. Sweat began to pour down me. 'Please, don't let me die out here tonight,' I heard myself say.

The footsteps came closer and voices got louder. I checked the door locks. I strained to hear what they were saying, trying to guess how many people were out there, if they'd bother to check out my battered old car. I picked up the knife I'd used earlier to spread the sardines. My hands shook as I fumbled about in the tray behind the gear stick for the car key. My fingers closed around it and I reached over to the steering wheel to slot it into the ignition. The footsteps paused and the voices hushed.

Still in my sleeping bag I hauled myself across to the driver's seat and, without turning on the lights and with my toes still inside the sleeping bag gripping the pedals, I turned the key in the ignition and drove straight off. Dark, shadowy figures stepped back against the bushes, but I couldn't see their faces behind the condensation on the windows. I made it to the road at the top without using lights or wipers, and almost without breathing. I'd escaped, I was alright! *Thank you, God.*

I parked somewhere else for a couple of nights after that, too scared to go back. But I always felt even more exposed anywhere else. Passing the laneway again one evening I saw that it was empty and parked up, drawn by its stillness and tranquillity. Maybe they wouldn't come back. I stayed awake the whole night, listening out for the sound of another car arriving. But it never did. So I went back night after night.

I got used to cars coming now and then after that, and having to move off for a few hours, or for a night. Occasionally, if they were parked far enough away, I would roll over in the sleeping bag and just lay there, my face pressed into the car seat, hoping whoever it was would reverse back out, but expecting to be showered with broken glass any second. But mostly, if I saw another car there when I arrived, or if any came later, I would just drive straight off, and wait somewhere else for a few hours before driving back. I didn't know what else to do or where else to go. I had to get stronger before I could face anything else. And apart from those times the only place I ever felt calm was when I was there, back in amongst the trees.

When I finally got back in touch with a case-worker at one of the homeless charities I'd phoned before Christmas, he apologised, saying he had been really busy. Again he promised that he'd phone me back when he had some news about deposits and rent in advance. And I promised to keep my phone on. Quite unrealistically, I was putting all my eggs in one basket again, waiting for that one call, not seeing beyond that. I'd told him I was living in my car, but I'm not sure he believed me. I only got in touch with them when I felt clear-headed and strong enough, so I probably never sounded like someone in all that much need. When he finally called back he said I wouldn't get the deposit and month in advance from anybody but if I tried to move into a homeless person's hostel I would have more chance of getting help and being able to move on from there. I told myself I couldn't do that because I would have to give up my car, but it was more because I was still in denial; I still wouldn't make myself visible enough to go to one. Anyway, I'd have to be mentally ill before I was likely to be offered a place in one, and mental illness was what I was trying to ward off. And the only way I knew to avoid that now was to stay in the calm of the trees.

Sleeping in the car during the summer was sometimes unbearably hot, even when I got to London at the beginning of September. Sometimes, even in the laneway at the beginning, I would have to lie for as long as possible with the door open, my legs hanging out, worried about heat-stroke but poised to lock myself back in if any people or foxes came. Gradually the months moved on to winter and when the cold finally set in I was stunned by it. And my life was soon reduced to simply overcoming the cold and getting through each day.

I would sleep in a hat and gloves and as many layers as I could inside the sleeping bag but would still wake up shivering, feeling as if there were slivers of ice floating about in my blood. But I still didn't know what else to do.

I had shut down. The position I was in was too over-whelming to even think about.

The cold penetrated every part of me: my teeth, my eyebrows, my chin, my hair, my sternum, the curve of my waist. It seemed to circle my tonsils, stiffen my eyeballs, hang from my lashes. It was everywhere: in my car seat, on my dashboard, in all my boxes and bags heaped up on the back seat. I couldn't escape it. It found its way to my kidneys, waking me almost hourly, forcing me out from under my, by then, warm layers into a brutally cold, pitch-black night to relieve myself yet again. I kept suffering nosebleeds from my right nostril, too, and I blamed that on the cold as well.

The heater in my car had never worked, but I couldn't afford to leave the engine running anyway, or to draw that much attention to my presence. I didn't want to die out there in the laneway, but each night, as winter tightened around me, I calmly accepted the possibility that I might – that one of those mornings I might simply not wake up.

Chapter 47

All the time in London I was still emailing off job applications. It was the main way I had of applying for jobs. I couldn't go to a Job Centre because I would have to tell them my address in London. Once they knew I was 'of no fixed abode' I thought I would have to queue up every week with all the other rough sleepers to get my benefit money, or get nothing at all. In the state of mind I was in, I was convinced that the only way I could survive, and get any strength back, was by staying as invisible as possible and that meant not getting recognised by other people, including other people sleeping rough like me. It was partly denial about my situation but also a survival tactic. It was also something deeply ingrained: a lifetime of secrets had made it hard to be publicly visible.

So I applied for jobs online, where only an email address is needed for contact details. I was registered with every job search site that I knew, and applied for dozens of jobs weekly, but they only ever resulted in one interview. It was for an administrator to work part-time in a woman's home. It meant I wouldn't have to dress up or worry about my appearance too much every day, and it made me think it would be possible to do it while living in the car for a while until I'd saved enough money to rent a room. I wanted it so much and was determined not to mess up the interview. I knew I had to make an effort with my appearance for that at least.

As soon as the launderette opened I washed my clothes so I would have time to iron them in a corner of the hospital when I went in to have my shower. I had an iron in one of the unopened bags in the boot of the car; I just needed a socket somewhere to plug it in. I spent half an hour frantically hurrying from place to place and floor to floor in the hospital looking for a socket in an unused corner somewhere that I could use discreetly. I was hoping to use the floor of the corridor as an ironing board, but every time I thought I had found the right spot, someone always appeared just as I was about to plug in the iron. I started to think I was hallucinating them, like I'd thought about the guy in the green dressing gown down near A & E.

I knew I couldn't give in to thinking like that, not if I was going to have any chance of getting this job and ending all this. I got the lift down to the basement and ran out to the car park. I had no idea what I was going to do. In the end I drove to a church I'd never been to before to ask if I could use a socket there. When it came to it I couldn't bear to tell the priest the truth about living in the car in case he turned me away, so I made up a story about having just come from the launderette, losing my door key and needing to iron something urgently for an interview. He was quite amused by my predicament and happily agreed to let me use his ironing board.

It hadn't left me much time to get to the interview but the woman had given me clear directions to her house and I was hopeful I'd make it. But on the way I got lost in roadwork diversions. Finally, twenty minutes after I was supposed to be there, I phoned to say I was just a few roads away and would be there any minute. She was justifiably annoyed and told me not to bother, as she needed someone reliable. I tried to convince her that it was the traffic, that I was reliable and would be there in five minutes at most, almost begging. She softened and agreed to see me, but I had trouble finding parking on any of the roads near hers. She had already said I could park on her driveway but there was no way I could let her see my car with all my possessions heaped up on the back seat, covered over with its faded black sheet. It was another twenty minutes before I got there.

It was raining heavily and I ran the three or four roads from the car to her house, with my bag over my head, trying to keep my hair dry, the rain splashing up my trouser legs. When she opened the door she looked me up and down and told me it was too late, that she had to go out for a meeting. I tried to persuade her to let me come back another time for another shot at it, but she must have seen the desperation in my eyes.

'I don't think so,' she said coldly, closing the door in my face. I walked away, feeling desolate, trying to swallow all the emotion that was threatening to come up. I could shut myself down almost at will by then. I drove back to the car park and spent the afternoon in a corner of Starbucks, just sitting there in the warmth, with my back to everyone, not thinking of it once, almost as if the whole incident hadn't happened. I spent a lot of time that winter sitting in a corner of Starbucks, hoping no one would realise I was homeless.

The experience confirmed one of my fears. I had worried for a long time that although my voice on the telephone still sounded respectable and my CV was impressive on some things, I no longer had the right 'image', and that when potential employers met me they would always be disappointed. I hadn't worked properly for almost two years by then, and with all this time sleeping rough in the car – my appearance getting shabbier and shabbier – I was already feeling unemployable. I didn't completely give up hope of a job, though. I couldn't; it was the only way out of my situation.

My other sleeping place, the one I drove off to at any sign of trouble, was a church car park I'd discovered was empty at night. It was surrounded by quiet streets of elegant Georgian houses. From where I usually parked in it I eventually realised I could see the old house of the therapist I'd visited for about eighteen months, almost ten years earlier. Sometimes, when the wind blew the branches aside, I could see the tall arched window lit up yellow at night, and through it the winding stairwell spiralling all the way up to the top floor. Giselle was the one person I'd told my entire background to, all the secrets of my childhood. Sitting there in the car at night waiting for it to be dark enough, or to brave the cold to get undressed, I'd find myself thinking of all the childhood stuff I had started to unwrap in the basement room of that house back then, and all those early memories would come back to me in thoughts or dreams.

Once, when I was very young and Brendan was taking me home one night, he stopped the car to watch the moon. It must have been somewhere along the Old Kent Road, a bright, straight road that seemed to go on forever in a very run-down area. I hadn't known he was my dad then. We sat in silence for ages, with the engine turning over, watching a big ivory moon in a black sky sail up over the rooftops.

Brendan was never much of a talker, but before we drove off he broke the silence by telling me that whenever I looked up and saw the moon he would be there, not far away, seeing it too, and to always think of that. 'Okay?' he said. I was already learning to shut myself off by then, and just sat on my hands and shrugged, continuing to stare right at the moon. I tried to tell him with my mind how much Mummy and I needed him there, my breathing like Morse code, turning to the window so that he couldn't see the emotion snag across my face.

I swallowed back the secrets I wasn't allowed to tell anyone and tried to keep the emotion from my voice and eyes as I shrugged again and told him that 'I don't need someone to be always there.'

The rest of that drive back was mostly silent. I pretended not to care about what he'd said. But in the wing mirror, I kept in my sight the big ivory moon that was following us all the way home; it was reassuring seeing it there around every turn.

And looking up through the windscreen at the moon night after night in the laneway, I often thought of Brendan and wished he'd phone me, or that I could phone him. But I could never tell him how I'd ended up living – if he could have helped me he would have done it back in Brighton. I knew I'd be in his thoughts, though, and seeing the moon he was never far from mine. It was like a constant reminder of him. It always had been.

Chapter 48

The day it all changed began like any other. I was sitting in the hospital canteen trying to make my cup of tea last as long as possible, wondering what I was going to do with myself for the rest of the day. As I tried to work out if I could afford another cup of tea, I noticed a rolled-up newspaper behind one of the water fonts and pulled it out. It was a Sunday paper and since I could never afford to buy newspapers I started reading it from cover to cover. One of the articles that grabbed my attention mentioned blogs. I had never heard of the word 'blog' before and only vaguely understood from the article what one was.

The next day, after checking emails in the library and sending my CV off for various jobs, I typed the word blog into a search engine and discovered that a blog was an online diary that could be read by anyone who came across it. Readers could respond to it too, leaving comments after each entry. I immediately liked the idea. It was a way of reaching out and communicating with people whilst remaining anonymous. Within minutes I discovered that a blog is free and simple to set up and run. Before I knew it I had created one of my own.

You have to choose a user name; off the top of my head I decided to call myself Wanderingscribe – I'm not sure why, a scribe is someone who writes and I had been wandering for a long time, so it seemed appropriate. I hadn't a clue what I was actually going to write – again it was something I hadn't planned; it just happened almost by accident, a bit like that first night sleeping in the car. You have to put a heading at the top of the blog where you describe it. Again I hadn't a clue what to put. I asked myself what I'd most want people to know about me in that moment. My fingers were already flying to the keys typing that I was 'homeless and living in my car, and desperate to find a way out of it'.

I couldn't believe I was actually admitting I was homeless to anyone who might come across my blog, but then at that stage I didn't actually think anyone would. I didn't have the courage or incentive to actually write an entry that day – to send any words out into the world. Besides, I had nothing to write. What could I say? I was homeless and I was totally ashamed of it. I saw it as completely failing in life, ending up in a position where I had nobody to go to, losing touch with people whenever I moved on, totally estranged from any family by then too. It was the last thing I could tell people in the 'real world', but maybe I'd be brave enough to tell people online in the 'virtual world' of the internet. It was almost a month before I found the courage to write in it, but once I did there was no stopping me. After all those months of isolation I'd found a way to communicate again.

In one of the first entries I struggled for ages to write the words 'I am homeless'. I couldn't understand why it was so hard to admit that, even to myself. Looking at the words on the screen, the sense of failure and shame made me feel physically ill.

Abandoned

On my blog I could be completely anonymous and honest about how I was living; I didn't have to try to cover it up as I was doing in my daily life. Sometimes I think I am better at writing than talking, and blogging was like a mixture of the two. Because there were soon real people reading the blog it gave it the immediacy and intimacy of face-to-face communication.

I hadn't spoken to anyone for months, not intimately anyway, so with the blog it felt like I was smashing down a wall back into the outside world, without exposing myself to any danger or embarrassment. I could tell people what was happening in my life and how I had become homeless without having to see the pity, disapproval or fear on their faces. For the first time in longer than I wished to remember, I could be real – maybe in some respects for the first time ever.

Almost straight away the blog started to give purpose to my days, becoming a reason to get out of the sleeping bag in the morning: to hurry off to see if anyone had left any comments or emails overnight. Complete strangers leaving messages saying 'Good morning, Scribe' and 'Keep your chin up today, Scribe' and 'Hang in there, Tiger'. I started writing in it daily. And very soon I wouldn't let anyone stop me from doing it, even when it seemed futile, even when some people online ridiculed my attempts to tell my story or dismissed my efforts to get out of my situation. For the first time in ages, something was driving me and I refused to listen to them. It was like something in me had switched back on. I was thinking positively again for the first time in what seemed like years.

* * *

Most people responded with kindness and encouragement to my situation, promising to pray for me and offering advice and assistance. I found it hard to respond, even though they made me feel connected and less alone, giving me some of the 'company' I hungered for, albeit at a safe distance online.

Once, early on, I almost met one particularly supportive woman for a coffee. She told me where she lived and it was quite close by. I liked the idea of spending some time with another woman after so many months of sitting in cafés on my own, making cups of tea last as long as possible, and trying to block out the sad songs blaring from the radios and the stares of other lonely people.

I noticed that the fifth email she had sent me came from what seemed like a man's address. Scrolling down, I found the address of a website which, when I checked it out, contained some very disturbing pornographic images. I felt confused and shocked. I emailed 'her' several times about it, but she didn't reply, leaving me feeling upset and far too freaked-out to meet her. I think I probably had a lucky escape. But it made me wary of ever meeting anyone else.

Despite this setback, the majority of the responses were giving me strength and perspective. All this time I had given in to negative thinking and now saw how wrong I had been to let Craig and my uncle win. I didn't deserve to be treated the way they had treated me. I didn't deserve to end up homeless, living in a car in a laneway. No one did. But all those months it was almost like I was punishing myself, saying I didn't fit in and didn't belong, making an outcast of myself, the way my uncle had all those years ago. Sometimes I shrunk to the size of a little girl.

Abandoned

The blog wasn't just about my homelessness; in fact it wasn't even about that a lot of the time. It wasn't about anything really; it was just a blog, a diary. There was such ugliness in my life and in people's reactions to me while I was homeless that I found writing in the blog often brought some beauty back into it; and sometimes that became the most important reason for doing it. Other times I wavered between just desperately wanting someone to realise I could still write and think rationally – despite what I was going through, and to give me a job to save me from the worse that was to come – and soon wanting to say some of the things that had been shut up in me for years. Although I wasn't ready, bits of information and splinters of memory would come out onto the screen from time to time.

I mentioned my childhood a few times in the blog, alluding to past traumas. This surprised me because I never intended to. I began to see that I had been deluding myself about any family still being there for me. They hadn't been there for years, but in my mind they were still family and I didn't know how to stop loving them.

Being in the car in the dark all those months had brought it all back. Vulnerable and alone and on the outside of everything, I sometimes felt like the little girl who had been sent out to stand in the kitchen in the dark. It felt like punishment in a way. The emotions it brought up in me were the same, too. As a child, under my uncle's abusive regime, I learned to cope with my emotions by shutting myself down to them. And that's how I coped with my emotions when I was living in my car, too. I was like a terrified child, trying to keep herself invisible so that no one would send her away. Writing the blog helped me

Abandoned

see that I'd been frightened of moving on. And realising
that finally allowed me to change the situation.

Chapter 49

W ithin a couple of months of starting it, my blog was stumbled upon by Ian Urbina, a journalist on *The New York Times*. He emailed me about an article he was doing on homelessness, and the moment I saw his email I had a feeling that this was somehow going to change things. After a series of emails and a meeting with one of his colleagues from their London office, he called and interviewed me by phone. He told me that I might end up not being mentioned in the article because it was about the 'hidden homeless' who live in their cars in America. But the internet does away with international boundaries.

The internet has taken the lid off the world, and blogs enable people — wherever they are in the world — to tell their stories. I was just a person reaching out to other people. It didn't really matter *where* in the world I was; I had a story to tell and through my blog I was putting it out there. Sometimes it felt close to prayer. I was living in a battered old car in an isolated laneway at the edge of some woods in England but I was a human being just like the rest, looking for a dignified way out of my situation. I had already received emails from people in America, Canada and Chile as well as all over Europe, who checked into my blog daily to see how I was doing. Those people were just as likely to offer a solution as the people I passed on the street every day.

A few weeks later, Ian Urbina's article appeared on the front page of the Sunday edition of *The New York Times* with a reference to my blog at the end of the article. There was also an audio interview with me included in the online edition. People all over the world seem to read the *NYT* online, and my Wanderingscribe blog went international overnight. Within hours I had hundreds of emails and comments from all corners of the world, giving support and advice about how to get out of the car and back into mainstream living.

Sean Coughlan, a BBC journalist, got in touch a few weeks later, having read the *NYT* article. He subsequently wrote an article about me on BBC News Online Magazine, and there was an overwhelming response from the media. Once the initial spate of thousands of hits after the *NYT* article died down, the blog was then receiving about 120 hits a day. But in the week after the BBC article was published it received over 48,000.

My luck eventually turned when one of the emails turned out to be from a literary agent who had looked at the blog after reading the BBC article. She invited me to a local café for coffee. As we chatted, she wanted to know a bit more about my background – how I'd ended up in the car and where my friends and family were. I told her the bare bones of my story and she eventually asked me whether I had considered writing a book about my experiences.

It was like a miracle. I could so easily have slipped through the net and ended up like the other people I had seen living and dying on the streets, but instead I was being offered a lifeline, a way back to the real world. It felt like I was waking up out of a nightmare straight into a dream.

Epilogue

Sometimes I can't believe this is over. I have to keep pinching myself.

I've found a place to live again now; somewhere I can start afresh and, I hope, in time put down roots. It's only a room in a shared house – a small, cream-walled room that still smells of new paint – not a place of my own. But it's a room with a door I can lock and curtains I can draw, and in many ways it is starting to feel like home already. After all this time of living in the car I finally have some privacy – no one staring in at me as they did through the windscreen as they walked down the laneway or past me on the street.

I have housemates again too, who are all friendly and relaxed and go out to work during the day. And I'm hopeful that soon I will be back out there with them. I am longing to throw myself into work again. But for now I'm relishing this time getting used to living indoors – being here where it is warm and clean and safe, and there are lots of plants and a big bath and shelves filled with books. I keep wandering in and out of the rooms just looking at things, picking objects up and putting them down again, finding the comfiest chairs, giving myself permission to be here.

Just propping a pillow against the headboard and lying back to read a book is an amazing feeling. For days I have pottered about doing nothing, feeling carpet under my toes, or standing barefoot on the cold tiles of the kitchen in the morning, eating toast dripping with butter and staring out at the early sky and down on the big horse chestnut tree in the neighbour's garden, amazed at how quiet it is from up here, even with the window open.

There's even a milkman who delivers, so there will always be milk for tea every morning. Even that makes me smile – knowing that I won't have to drive off somewhere every morning to get it in a polystyrene cup, or pay over a pound for it, or drink it out on the street somewhere. It's the small things I can't get over.

I dreamed of doing so many things when this moment came: taking a long bubble bath with music in the background and a glass of wine in my hand; watching TV; cooking the food I'd fantasised about all those months. But on my first night I was too tired and just fell into a deep sleep. It will take a while for my body to get used to lying straight, to realise it can uncurl and slowly release some of the pain. But I know it will happen.

I had slipped into another world and started to fear that I would never find a way out. I understand why so many people turn to drink, drugs or crime to blot out the reality of homelessness – it's almost impossible to live it and experience it at the same time; you have to detach from the harshness and the loneliness of it somehow. I really thought I had come to the end of the line. I couldn't have imagined getting back to where I was before. I know it will be a difficult road ahead as I readjust and come to terms with everything that has happened, but everything feels possible again, and I'm feeling positive.

I've even had the courage to get back in touch with some of my friends from the past and have been amazed by how supportive they have been. None of them have judged me badly. I'm also back in touch with Brendan. I finally plucked up the courage to call him and have even been over to see him to explain about this book and how it came about. I haven't told him everything about how I ended up living yet but quite surprisingly he has been the most supportive of all in me writing this book. So he will find out when he reads it. I hope Mummy and Kathy come back into my life one day too. I hope they'll see that this isn't a book about blame. Neither, apart from the abuse, is it about anyone doing anything wrong. It's about people making mistakes and trying to make the best of the situation. It's about being human, about falling and picking yourself up again.

The room is still full of my bags and boxes. It's taking me a while to bring myself to open them, to have the courage to put things on shelves and away in drawers. To find a place for even the smallest possession is emotional in ways I hadn't expected. I'm doing it slowly, bag by bag, evening by evening, finding everything a home – somewhere to belong.

It's hard to believe there will be no more cold nights sleeping in pain with my head against the car doors; no owls calling through the trees at night or foxes wailing; no birds keeping me awake at five in the morning; no rain blowing in through the unsealed car windows, or other cars turning up in the pitch dark. I shiver when I think of it – it's only now that the reality of all the dangers I faced every night is starting to hit me.

My first instinct was to hide all the evidence of my homelessness – to start afresh, burn my boots and put down new roots – to have nothing more to do with the way I was living. But I keep reminding myself that there is nothing to be ashamed of in how I ended up. Lives unravel. People don't, or won't, keep up for all sorts of reasons and have to find other ways of living all the time. I am not the first and I won't be the last. And although my life felt over many times in the last year, I now see how lucky I have been all along. I had almost given up, but it seems that life *is* full of second chances after all.

Yes, I have been very lucky, and I won't ever forget that. So many times in the car, when I expected things to go wrong, they didn't. Something always turned up. But it's more than just luck.

When I was in the car I used to feel I had a guardian angel watching over me. Sometimes, when walking away from the car, leaving it there with all my bags and boxes heaped up on the back seat, I would imagine a pair of angels standing either side of it. And I knew it would be safe, everything still there when I got back. Glancing over my shoulder as I turned to walk out of sight, I would see their huge, radiant, white-feathered wings draped across the green, mud-streaked roof, shielding it. Last night I imagined them here, with me, in this room.

The bed still felt huge after so long in the cramped inside of my car, and as I rolled over half-asleep in the luxury of a warm duvet I felt tiny, like that little girl again. And I imagined them whispering down to her, 'You did it, little Anya, you made it, you survived.'

* * *

If you want to read Anya's blog, or start your own, go to: http://wanderingscribe.blogspot.com